'More than a language…'

NIACE Committee of Inquiry on English for Speakers of Other Languages

Final report

October 2006

Contents

Section

References

Annexes

Preface

At a time of rapid industrial and demographic change, hundreds of thousands of people have migrated to the UK to fill vacant jobs. Many thousands of them need improved English language skills to contribute effectively. They join the hundreds of thousands of Britain's settled communities who also need strengthened English language skills to participate fully in society at large, and at work. The combination of demand has overwhelmed what was already overstretched supply, and makes clear the need to look afresh at how we best make provision to meet these needs. There is also a disturbing and disagreeable underbelly in British polity that blames foreigners for their 'foreignness', and fails to recognise the enrichment of our lives that cultural diversity brings. The negative strain also fails to recognise the major economic contribution settled refugees and migrants make. It is a mark of civilisation where countries offer asylum to people whose lives have been dislocated by war, famine and social chaos. Giving English language skills to migrants, refugees and asylum seekers alike makes economic and social sense.

NIACE, the National Institute of Adult Continuing Education, established an inquiry into English for speakers of other languages (ESOL) to contribute a fresh look at the issues. Its recommendations are wide-ranging and challenging, and I am happy to commend them to government departments, employers, and providers alike.

As this report makes clear, English language learning has an impact on individuals, communities and the productivity and safety of workplaces in England. For individuals it makes a difference to the way we relate to each other and it impacts on our children. Without doubt there is for many a correlation between their self-esteem and the level of confidence they have in spoken English. For many, confidence in English language opens doors and helps people engage in and contribute to civil society. Lack of fluency in the language condemns many people to poverty. ESOL is both a subject in its own right and a means to an end for individuals. English language is a recognised route to citizenship, and language competency is now a requirement. At the societal level, the opportunity to improve English language should be a right; a chance to contribute to and at the same time shape the communities in which we live and work.

In the workplace ESOL can make the difference between a confident and skilled workforce and one that is hesitant or exploited, where individuals are at risk of missing opportunities, and in some contexts at risk for their lives. It can make a difference to economic development and to the effectiveness of services and companies. Good communication is always at the heart of what employers say they need from employees, and it is a pre-condition for flexible, responsive and competitive enterprises. Without it, there is less opportunity for all. In short, ESOL is more than a language; it is both a language and a skill for life.

This is the final report of the NIACE Committee of Inquiry on English for Speakers of Other Languages (ESOL). The major concerns highlighted in the Interim Report remain. Our executive summary highlights these major concerns and some of the recommendations which the Committee believes will begin to address them. I am grateful to Derek Grover CB for his work in chairing the Committee and drafting the report, and to the Committee members for their hard work. I am also grateful to the support team at NIACE: Jane Ward, Peter Lavender, Giustine Kettle and Yanina Dutton, who have helped the Committee and the Chair to produce what I think is a very clear report. Thank you all.

Alan Tuckett
Director, NIACE

Introduction, executive summary and summary of recommendations

Executive summary

Introduction

2.1 This report provides an overview of the major challenges affecting the provision of English language teaching for speakers of other languages (ESOL).[1] It is based on evidence, written and oral, submitted to our committee,[2] a study of the relevant documents and on discussion in the five meetings which the committee has held. It is the first comprehensive overview of policy on ESOL since the Department for Education and Skills (DfES) committee which produced *Breaking the Language Barriers* in 2000.

2.2 The situation described in this report gives serious cause for concern. Over the last six years there has been very significant investment of public funds in ESOL provision. In the 2004–5 academic year the Learning and Skills Council (LSC) spent £279 million on ESOL funding which provided 538,700 ESOL learning opportunities. Effective ESOL is critical to empowering adults to gain independence and control over their lives, to increasing social inclusion and cohesion and to the country's skills agenda. It is also of increasing importance to a wide range of key government policies, including community regeneration, combating racism, improving health and housing, as well as the obvious areas of education and skills. Demand for ESOL provision is rising, in part from migrant workers from the new members of the European Union, but also from refugees and there is significant unmet demand from members of settled communities. Despite the substantial investment, funding is not always well targeted to those in greatest need, and the quality of provision is worryingly patchy, with too much sub-standard provision. In some parts of the country there are not enough qualified teachers, and the structure of ESOL teaching qualifications is in urgent need of the reform which is now under way.

2.3 Our recommendations are designed to address this situation. We believe that policy development and planning of the delivery of ESOL should be coordinated across the full range of government policies and the full range of providers. We recommend a series of actions to ensure that there is more ESOL provision effectively targeted on the world of work. We recommend a coherent package of activities designed to address the most significant quality issues, including important concerns about the recently introduced qualifications for learners. We welcome the work being done on ESOL teacher qualifications and make some further suggestions which we believe will help improve teacher supply and quality. Finally we recognise that the present funding situation is not sustainable and make recommendations which are designed to target resource on those learners and potential learners most in need, and to increase the range of funding sources available to support ESOL provision. Some of our recommendations are somewhat technical: we make no apology for that, as careful attention to the realities of the provision which is made on the ground is essential to secure real and lasting improvements. These

---

[1] The Committee used a broad definition of ESOL to include all English language provision and support for adult speakers of other languages.
[2] The sources of evidence to our committee are set out in Annexe 2.

recommendations are intended to be a coherent package and we commend them to the government, the funding bodies, the organisations responsible for the learning infrastructure, and to the providers, public and private, of ESOL.

Summary

2.4   ESOL provision is critically important to the UK. It is essential to help secure social inclusion and help build stable and successful communities, and it underpins current policy on citizenship and settlement. It is also critical to policies on skills. There will not be enough young people coming on to the labour market to meet all the demands for new and changed skills which are foreseen. The shortfall will have to be met by retraining adults and by migrants. Skills acquisition by both these groups has to be underpinned by good ESOL provision. But the impact of effective ESOL provision goes wider than this. Language skills are also critical to the success of a range of other key government policies, including the child poverty agenda, health, sustainable communities, regeneration, and community integration and cohesion, including refugee integration.

2.5   This wider relevance makes it essential that ESOL provision is planned and delivered across the full range of relevant policies and activities, not considered separately in each of the relevant contexts. There should be a fundamental cross-government review of ESOL as part of the forthcoming Comprehensive Spending Review. A minister should be appointed to lead the implementation of its conclusions. The DfES should set up a national advisory forum on ESOL to ensure that policy developments across government take full account of ESOL, and the LSC should set up local fora for the planning of ESOL delivery across the full range of providers in each locality.

2.6   Since the introduction of the *Skills for Life* policy, ESOL has been viewed as part of that programme. It has taken an increasingly large proportion of *Skills for Life* funding, and it is clear that this is of concern to policy makers. ESOL has both benefited and suffered from its position within the wider policy. It has undoubtedly benefited from a higher level of policy attention and from greatly increased funding, and that is very welcome. But ESOL goes wider than adult literacy, since it has elements both of a basic skill and of foreign language learning and levels go above the Level 2 threshold. Pedagogy, funding regimes, targets, and standards and qualifications which are, quite properly, designed mainly for literacy and numeracy learners are being applied in an ESOL context to which they are not entirely appropriate. This issue underpins a number of the current difficulties with ESOL provision. In developing policy and provision in the future, it is essential that ESOL is considered as a distinct element of the wider policy and that, where necessary, adjustments to infrastructure and delivery are made to meet the needs of English language learners.

2.7   Demand for ESOL is high and growing. The increased demand from migrant workers, especially from the A8 countries, has attracted much publicity and it is undoubtedly significant. But such learners, and refugees and asylum seekers, are only one element, although a growing element, of current ESOL learners. There are also increasing demands from the settled communities. One consequence of this changing pattern is that there are now demands in some areas, particularly rural, which have not hitherto experienced high demand for ESOL provision and which do not have the infrastructure of providers or teachers to cope. So far as migrant workers are concerned, mechanisms should be found to ensure that the employers who recruit them should take some responsibility for ensuring that they have adequate English language skills. Our recommendations on funding are designed to help cope with this increasing demand by focusing the available resource more sharply on those in most need, and by increasing the contributions made by learners themselves and by employers.

2.8   ESOL provision has a key role in promoting social inclusion. The link to citizenship is established in legislation, and it is clearly essential that enough high quality ESOL is available to people who wish to acquire citizenship or qualify for settlement. ESOL is particularly important in addressing issues of intergenerational learning and the agenda on early years policy set out in *Every Child Matters*. There should be a review of the role of ESOL in these policies, and specifically there should be an increase in the funding of ESOL related to family learning. ESOL is also important to enable people to play a full role in civic and cultural life and contribute to their local communities. The current state of ESOL in custodial settings is a matter of great concern: the improvements planned are welcome but they will not have an impact unless they are pursued vigorously and consistently in a planned and monitored programme.

2.9   Many ESOL learners are mainly motivated by a wish to gain work, or to progress at work. Progress in developing provision which links vocational and ESOL learning has been slow, and we have recommended a number of steps which would speed up progress in this area. The LSC has recently taken over responsibility from Jobcentre Plus (JCP) for employability-related ESOL programmes for the unemployed. It is worrying to note that one consequence of this transfer appears to be that the resource available for this vulnerable group of learners has been sharply reduced. The LSC and JCP are reported to be working together on a new programme for this target group: it is essential that it should have both employability and learning outcomes, and that it should be available for lower-level learners, not just those learners who count towards the LSC's current Public Service Agreement (PSA) targets. It is also essential that ways are found of building on the successful ESOL Pathfinder projects involving employers, and of encouraging employers to contribute to the costs of meeting the ESOL needs of their employees. All Sector Skills Councils (SSCs) need to become more involved in this agenda, and it should also form part of the work of Regional Skills Partnerships and Regional Skills Strategies.

2.10   Evidence from inspections makes it clear that too little ESOL provision is good or better, and that there is still too much that is inadequate. A concerted approach is required to tackle this. There should be a thematic inspection of ESOL by the Adult Learning Inspectorate (ALI) and the Office for Standards in Education (Ofsted), complemented by a continuation of the valuable National Research and Development Centre for Adult Literacy and Numeracy (NRDC) research programme. New ESOL qualifications have only recently been introduced and the new framework has been widely welcomed. It will be essential to make an early assessment of their success, in terms of take-up and their impact on learners, teachers and providers, not least because some worries are already being expressed about their suitability. Alongside this evaluation, it is essential that the new qualifications are promoted to learners, employers, further and higher education and the professions. It will also be important to reconsider the way in which qualifications are used in relation to the funding system. The current discrepancy between the funding of ESOL and literacy qualifications, which is driven by the structure of the funding regime, should be corrected. Guidance should be produced on how best to implement the Individual Learning Plan (ILP) approach in the ESOL context, taking account of ESOL pedagogy and the needs and capabilities of English language learners.

2.11   Because of their often difficult personal circumstances ESOL learners frequently turn to the providers of their learning for support with concerns relevant to their wider lives. Many ESOL teachers deal with these issues with great dedication and skill, even though it is beyond their responsibilities. But it is essential to ensure that all ESOL teachers are aware of these wider issues and, even if they do not tackle them themselves, know how to get effective help for their learners. More work needs to be done on how best to provide this wider support in the learning context. It is also essential that other professionals dealing with the relevant communities are aware of ESOL issues and how to enable their clients to get access to appropriate provision. It would be helpful if the current DfES-sponsored review of information, advice and guidance could specifically consider the needs of ESOL learners. Learners who are disabled or who have learning difficulties face particular challenges: it is important that ESOL teachers are given an opportunity to learn about and discuss the new guidelines on disability. We also believe that it is important to continue development work on the use of ICT in ESOL teaching and we look forward to the practitioner guide which NRDC are to produce in this area.

2.12 Dealing with the wide variety of learners and the range of provision undoubtedly presents major challenges to the leadership and management of providers. It is important that senior leaders and managers have awareness of the particular challenges of ESOL and there should be effective continuing professional development (CPD) in place to promote this. There is an important role here for the Centre for Excellence in Leadership (CEL).

2.13 Implementing our recommendations would add up to a formidable programme of work, in addition to the costs of meeting increasing demand. Simply asking for more money for more of the same is not a sensible option. In these circumstances we do not believe that the current arrangements for funding ESOL are sustainable. We need to look for ways of increasing the streams of funding available to support ESOL learning while targeting public funding on those in greatest need.

2.14 In the immediate future there is a particular issue about the entitlements to free learning available to ESOL learners and those available to literacy and numeracy learners. In effect free provision is available to eligible learners below Level 2. We would not argue that this position can be sustained in the long term, but it would be unacceptable to remove that entitlement from ESOL learners while retaining it for literacy and numeracy. Such a course of action would be unfair and discriminatory. For the same reasons it would not be right to introduce a means-tested regime for ESOL learners alone. But when the system of entitlements for literacy and numeracy learners is reviewed it would be right to review it for ESOL learners too. A better-targeted system might have the following main characteristics:

- All people with ESOL needs should have the right to a free initial assessment of up to three hours. This helps ensure that people are directed to appropriate provision.

- All ESOL learners with language skills below Level 1 should be entitled to free provision until they have reached that level.

- Above Level 1 provision should be paid for at vocational rates, with remissions available for those in financial need.

- These arrangements should be underpinned by a loan scheme for those who need it, aimed particularly at those with high-level learning needs.

- If the immediate entitlement of asylum seekers to free ESOL provision is withdrawn, asylum seekers should have the same entitlements as EU migrants when the target period for decision on their application has expired, or when their application has been granted. We recognise that this may well happen before a wider revision of the system.

- Spouses, fiancées and family members of permanent UK residents should have immediate access to the same entitlements to ESOL provision as permanent residents. This too could happen before a wider revision.

- Employers and agencies recruiting workers from abroad should be obliged to contribute to the cost of their acquiring language skills up to Level 1.

2.15 It is essential that the funding arrangements, both short and long term, can support the full range of provision that is required by learners. It is essential that local LSCs are reminded that Entry Level 1 and 2 provision leading to nationally approved qualifications is fundable, and that one of the objectives of their purchasing strategy for ESOL should be to achieve a balanced portfolio of provision with clear progression routes available for learners. So far as higher-level training is concerned, the loan scheme we have recommended, which would require some underpinning from public funds, would help, but we believe that those employers, such as the NHS, which place particular reliance on immigrants with higher-level skills, should contribute to these costs.

2.16 This is a radically different approach to funding ESOL, but we believe it would use the public money available more effectively, be fairer to learners, and ensure that the system can make the full range of provision required to provide the ESOL needed to meet important national objectives.

Conclusion

2.17 This report makes it clear that having a successful system of ESOL is of fundamental importance to this country. But there are significant issues to be addressed if we are to meet that challenge. This report sets out a package of recommendations which we believe would have a major positive impact, and we hope that government, funders, infrastructure bodies and providers will respond positively to it. This is not a challenge that, as a nation, we can afford to shirk.

Summary of recommendations

(Corresponding paragraph numbers are shown after each recommendation.)

1   There should be a cross-departmental review of the current provision of, and future need for, ESOL across the full range of government policies and expenditure on it in the context of the forthcoming Comprehensive Spending Review.   `3.12`

2   The Learning and Skills Council (LSC) should take the lead in setting up regional planning fora to implement the coordinated policies for ESOL agreed at national level.   `3.12`

3   A ministerial lead on ESOL should be identified with a specific brief to address ESOL issues across the full range of government policies, and to ensure implementation across government of the Comprehensive Spending Review study.   `3.12`

4   The Department for Education and Skills (DfES) should review the implementation of the *Skills for Life* strategy to ensure that ESOL is given appropriate attention and priority.   `3.17`

5   The DfES should convene a national advisory group or forum on ESOL to act as a source of expertise and advice on ESOL issues and to ensure that policy developments across government take full account of ESOL issues.   `3.21`

6   Work-related language training for migrants, refugees and the members of settled communities should be addressed in Regional Economic Strategies and the work of Regional Strategic Partnerships.   `5.15`

Social inclusion

7   The DfES should ensure that the links with ESOL policy, provision and providers have been effectively made in relation to each of the key aspects of the implementation of *Every Child Matters* and the 14–19 strategy.   `4.16`

8   The DfES and appropriate partners should commission a national programme to develop, test and disseminate models and materials for ESOL to support civic and democratic participation.   `4.18`

9   The planned improvements to ESOL for offenders in custodial and community settings should be pursued actively in a planned and monitored programme, if the current deplorable state of ESOL for offenders is the be remedied.   `4.21`

ESOL and work

10 The DfES and appropriate partners should commission two development programmes: first, to identify and disseminate effective models and funding approaches for assisting learners with English language learning needs to succeed on vocational programmes; and second, to draw out and disseminate the lessons from English language and employability programmes. These developments should be explicitly prioritised in funding and planning guidance.   `5.8` `5.9`

11 The design of the new LSC employability and ESOL programme should take into account the distinctive needs of ESOL learners, and have both learning and employability outcomes, and ensure that the learning outcomes should address the needs of Entry Level learners as well as higher-level learners who count towards the LSC's current Public Service Agreement (PSA) targets.   `5.11`

12 The Quality Improvement Agency (QIA) should commission the development of a curriculum and related materials for workplace-related ESOL and related teacher training materials.   `5.17`

Quality

13 The Adult Learning Inspectorate (ALI) and the Office for Standards in Education (Ofsted) should undertake a national survey inspection on the quality of ESOL which would analyse existing reports and undertake field visits, with a view to making recommendations, taking into account the recommendations of this Committee.   `6.3`

14 The National Research and Development Centre for Adult Literacy and Numeracy (NRDC) should be commissioned to continue and extend its programme of research and development work on ESOL as an essential complement to the thematic inspection of ESOL which we have recommended.   `6.4`

15 The impact of the new ESOL learner qualifications should be assessed, and the DfES and the Qualifications and Curriculum Authority (QCA) should consider how best to promote them to learners, employers, higher education and the professions.   `6.13`

16 The disparity between the assessment of literacy and ESOL qualifications in relation to the national *Skills for Life* targets should be corrected.   `6.15`

17 The appropriateness for ESOL learners, particularly at lower levels, of the Individual Learning Plan (ILP) process should be reviewed.   `6.21`

18 The current DfES review of information, advice and guidance (IAG) services should urgently look at the needs of ESOL learners.   `6.29`

19   The Matrix standards should require that candidates who advise ESOL learners are properly briefed and trained to enable them to respond knowledgeably and effectively to their specific circumstances and requirements. We also recommend that the survey inspection proposed by the Committee should examine in particular how appropriately skilled and qualified learning assistants, learning support workers and teaching assistants can be used effectively to support programmes.   `6.29`

20   There should be training for ESOL teachers on the new guidance on disability and how effectively to share assessment strategies in relation to ESOL learners with learning difficulties or disabilities across their organisations.   `6.31`

Teacher training

21   As pre-service training routes to employment are introduced, employers should be actively discouraged from employing new ESOL teachers who are unqualified.   `7.11`

22   Consideration should be given to offering small amounts of core funding support to appropriate voluntary professional support organisations and peer group networks to enable them to maintain and expand their provision of continuing professional development (CPD). Ways should also be developed of helping colleges and other providers to share expertise.   `7.16`

23   Progress towards introduction of the new qualifications for teachers should be kept under close scrutiny. If there is any danger that they cannot be fully and effectively implemented to the current timetable, urgent consideration should be given to extending the cut-off date for teacher training courses meeting the current standards, to avoid a lacuna of courses for teachers in September 2007.   `7.13`

24   Incentives should be introduced to encourage employers to introduce a more secure career structure for ESOL teachers and increase the proportion of teachers employed on permanent contracts.   `7.19`

25   The Higher Education Funding Council for England (HEFCE) and the LSC should consider the level at which they are prepared to fund ESOL teacher training, to ensure that the new qualifications include high quality teaching practice placements in a range of learning contexts, with support from ESOL specialist teacher trainers and mentors.   `7.21`

26   Guidelines to Local Education Authorities (LEAs) on means-tested maintenance grants and funding guidelines for teachers taking ESOL teacher-training courses should be clarified.   `7.22`

27   The Centre for Excellence in Leadership (CEL) should undertake work on professional development relating to ESOL for college managers at all levels.   `8.7`

28   ESOL should be more specifically addressed in the national quality improvement strategy for *Skills for Life*, funded by the QIA.   `8.8`

Funding and entitlements

29 One of the objectives of the funding arrangements for ESOL should be to ensure a varied network of high-quality providers. `6.5`

30 The guidance to local LSCs should make it clear that Entry Level 1 and 2 provision leading to nationally approved qualifications is fundable, a sub-target for Entry Level 2 should be introduced and one of the objectives of their purchasing strategy for ESOL should be to achieve a balanced portfolio of provision with clear progression routes available for learners. `9.12`

31 If the immediate entitlement of asylum seekers to free ESOL provision is withdrawn, asylum seekers should have the same entitlements as home learners when the target period for decision on their application has expired. `9.18`

32 Spouses, fiancées and family members of permanent UK residents should have immediate access to the same entitlements to ESOL provision as permanent residents. `9.19`

33 When the current *Skills for Life* entitlements are revised, all ESOL learners with language skills below Level 1 should be entitled to free provision until they have reached that level. `9.25`

34 There should be an increase to the LSC's Personal and Community Development budget to support an increase in family ESOL programmes, aimed specifically at increasing opportunities for women from under-represented ethnic minority communities. `9.25`

35 All adults with ESOL requirements should have the right to a free initial assessment of up to three hours. `9.26`

36 The government should explore the development of a subsidised loan scheme for individuals not entitled to further free provision who wish to undertake ESOL learning beyond their basic entitlement, especially for higher-level learning. `9.28`

37 The Department of Trade and Industry (DTI) should make it a condition of granting licences to employment agencies recruiting from EU countries that they should, at their expense, ensure that their workers are enabled to secure adequate English language skills, whether in their country of origin or in the UK. `9.29`

38 The new criteria for the designation of A-rated sponsors for non-EU migrant workers should include the provision of appropriate ESOL training. `3.25`

39 The government should ensure that employers secure ESOL provision for their workers, whether from migrant or settled communities. To support the measures recommended in 37, 38 and 39 it is crucial that regulatory and enforcement measures are adopted to ensure employers are prevented from transferring costs to workers, including migrant workers, and ensure the exploitation of migrant workers does not increase. `9.29`

What is ESOL and why is it important?

In this section we argue that because ESOL is critical to the success of a wide range of government policies it is essential that policy and delivery are coordinated nationally, regionally and locally across government and the responsible agencies. ESOL should remain part of the Skills for Life programme but the distinctive needs of ESOL learners should be more fully recognised in policy development and delivery. The demand for ESOL is changing, with significant new demands from migrant workers, especially from the A8 countries, alongside continuing demand for ESOL from settled communities. Current funding does not allow all these needs to be met: a revision to funding arrangements to target resources on those most in need is therefore required.

3.1   The central argument of this report is that ESOL is an issue of key importance not just in terms of education and skills policy but also in terms of much wider policy. We believe that current policy does not adequately acknowledge or address those wider issues, and much current practice and thinking is driven by an out-of-date and inappropriate model of ESOL. Paradoxically, at a time when much, very welcome, extra resource has been devoted to ESOL it has increasingly been treated as an element (albeit a very large and increasing element) of wider policy on literacy, language and numeracy (skills for life) and effectively submerged in the infrastructure, targets and funding mechanisms developed to implement the *Skills for Life* policy. The distinctive nature of ESOL, the differences between mainstream *Skills for Life* learners and ESOL learners and their wide range of needs have not been given enough weight in programme design and implementation. We do not believe this position is sustainable, and argue that we need major changes in policy and practice if we are to meet the demands likely to be placed in the system in the short to medium term. This section of the report sets out our best view of the likely future demands on the system, and why we believe that it is important that they are met. This report deals with adult learners: while our main focus is on learners aged 19+, many of the points we make apply also to younger learners.

3.2   There can be little argument about the importance of ESOL to the life chances of individual learners and to supporting the valuable contribution they can make to the social, economic, and cultural life of the nation. English language skills are recognised in both policy and research outcomes as the essential underpinning of social integration and of labour market success. Immigrants with fluent English language skills are 20 per cent more likely to be in employment and earn approximately 20 per cent more than those with underdeveloped language skills (Bloch, 2002; Dustmann and Fabbri, 2003). It is important not to draw a sharp and artificial distinction between economic and social aims. The point is well expressed in the 1998 White Paper *The Learning Age*:

> *As well as securing our economic future, learning has a wider contribution. It helps make ours a civilised society, develops the spiritual side of our lives and promotes active citizenship. Learning enables people to play a full part in their community. It strengthens the family, the neighbourhood and consequently the nation.* (DfEE, 1998)

3.3 We believe that this generous and inclusive vision of the purposes of learning applies with particular force to ESOL learning. The importance of language to citizenship, democratic participation, social cohesion and integration is clearly recognised in current policy. To take one example, current legislation requires applicants for naturalisation to show a sufficient knowledge of language and life in the UK. It is clear that this policy can only succeed if supported by well-planned, well-targeted and well-delivered ESOL provision.

3.4 While the social benefits of English language skills are self-evident, it is not so clear that the wider economic significance of ESOL is fully recognised. As the recent interim report by Lord Leitch points out, two in three of the new jobs which will be created in the next ten years cannot be filled by young people because there will not be enough entering the labour market (Leitch, 2005). The only alternative sources of labour to fill these jobs will be adults and migrant workers. The contribution made by migrants to our economic prosperity has been substantial in the past and will inevitably increase over the next decade. The question is whether the extent and the nature of ESOL provision are adequate for it to play its key role in optimising that contribution.

3.5 The importance of the economic dimension can already be seen in the sharp increase in demand for ESOL provision from migrant workers,[3] many from the A8 countries.[4] Their presence in the UK is essentially the direct result of labour market demand. Refugees also make an important contribution to the labour market, although they could contribute more if they were enabled to access employment that utilises the full range of their training, skills and experience. Asylum seekers have many skills to offer, although they are not allowed to work whilst waiting for a decision on their applications. Better targeted and more effective ESOL provision would have a major impact in helping learners work to their full potential, with obvious benefits to individuals but also with wider benefits in terms of an improved stock of skills in the labour market and thus greater labour market flexibility. Even in entry-level jobs, lack of English language skills restricts productivity and may lead to bad health and safety practices.

3.6 It is important to set this issue in the wider context of current policy on skills, which is based on a commitment to improve national productivity through improving skills. It focuses on upgrading the vocational and basic skills of low-skilled and unemployed adults, and reaffirms the government's commitment to helping people improve literacy, language and numeracy (LLN) skills. The prime focus is progression to the Level 2 functional skills that are seen as 'employability skills.' But it is questionable whether a focus on Level 2 is an adequate response to the needs of all ESOL learners, many of whom have qualifications and work experience well above Level 2, and in particular whether it will enable them to maximise their potential participation in the labour market and hence the benefits they bring to the UK. As the Leitch review's interim report demonstrates, the rate of return to improving higher-level skills is substantial in terms of economic and social benefits (Leitch, 2005). Investment in improving the English language skills of migrants with higher-level vocational skills would be a cost-effective way of maximising the contribution they were able to make to national economic prosperity.

3.7 These are significant arguments in favour of investment in ESOL provision. But the importance of ESOL goes wider: just as it is central to the life chances of individual learners, so it is central to a wide range of policy issues. As the committee chaired by Lord Moser to consider adult basic skills identified, poor basic skills[5] have a direct link to social and economic disadvantage, including high levels of unemployment or employment at low skill levels, intergenerational educational underachievement, high levels of crime, poor

---

[3] There are many understandings of the term 'migrant worker'. It is used here to refer to all adults living in the UK for employment purposes. Currently in Home Office documents it refers to people who come to the UK to work (of whom all non-EU citizens need visas, and for whom the employer needs a work permit).

[4] The eight Eastern European states that joined the European Union in May 2004 are known collectively as the A8 states, and nationals of these states now have free movement of labour in the UK.

[5] The term 'basic skills' used when this report was published has been replaced by the more specific 'literacy, language and numeracy'.

health, poor housing and low levels of civic participation (Moser, 1999). For ESOL learners these issues are too frequently compounded by their experiences of discrimination and racism. Addressing basic skills issues, Moser concluded, would be an essential component of policies to tackle these issues. As the Social Exclusion Unit report *Improving Services, Improving Lives* demonstrates, adequate levels of literacy, language and numeracy (LLN), and in particular literacy, are key to the effective delivery of public services to the most disadvantaged (ODPM, 2005).

3.8 Both these studies are concerned with LLN, with the main focus on literacy and numeracy. But many of their conclusions apply also to ESOL learners for whom the issues of education and health, work, immigration, settlement, integration, citizenship, neighbourhood renewal, combating racism and community cohesion are particularly relevant, but currently are rarely specifically considered in relation to learning provision.

3.9 The important message from these and many other research studies and policy papers is that areas that may appear in terms of policy or service delivery to be distinct are in practice inextricably linked, not least in the lives and experiences of the service users themselves. This presents important issues for both policy and delivery.

3.10 The issue for policy makers is to recognise and take into account the extent to which effective language skills are a precondition of success in many key policy areas. We have cited above the case of citizenship, an example where the importance of language skills is explicitly acknowledged, but arguably not adequately taken into account in current planning and funding arrangements. A failure to plan adequate ESOL provision leads to delays in applications for naturalisation, which means that the naturalisation programme cannot proceed as planned. Other policy areas for which language skills are important include the child poverty agenda, health, sustainable communities, regeneration, and community integration and cohesion, including refugee integration (cf. DWP, 2005; Home Office, 2005b).

3.11 The issue for funders and providers is to ensure that services are planned, funded and delivered in a coherent way which responds to the full range of ESOL learners' needs. This is not simply an issue of aligning curriculum to the wider needs of learning (as in the example of ESOL citizenship materials mentioned above) although this can be an effective and important strategy. It is a matter of consistently aligning policy development, planning and funding streams for ESOL learning and delivery with the programmes of the other organisations dealing with these learners. The aim is to provide services which the users themselves experience as joined-up and mutually reinforcing. At the least, where English language is seen as an essential underpinning of work in other policy areas, coherent planning on these lines would prevent policy makers in one area making incorrect assumptions about the availability, scale or nature of ESOL provision, and at best would ensure that provision is available to equip people to engage effectively, contribute to society and benefit from the full range of opportunities and services available. The opportunity is there to make a major improvement of the full range of services to some very disadvantaged groups. Local Area Agreements could provide a framework for this at local level.

3.12 We believe that these issues need to be addressed both at the level of national policy making and on the ground. The forthcoming Comprehensive Spending Review presents an excellent opportunity to begin this process at the highest level of planning. **We recommend that there should be a cross-departmental review of the current provision of, and future need for, ESOL across the full range of government policies and expenditure on it in the context of the forthcoming Comprehensive Spending Review (CSR).** It is clear that more effective coordination at local level will also be essential to make a reality on the ground of any closer integration of policy at national level. **We recommend that the LSC should take the lead in setting up regional planning fora to implement the coordinated policies for ESOL agreed at national level.** These fora will need to involve all the agencies and organisations which plan and fund ESOL provision and should link to the Regional Skills Partnerships.

Their work should be reflected in regional skills strategies. We also believe that, while it is important to acknowledge the relevance of ESOL to a wide range of policy issues, it is essential that there is a clear lead responsibility within government to ensure the coherence of policy and to ensure that ESOL issues are always taken into account in wider policy making. **We recommend that a ministerial lead on ESOL should be identified with a specific brief to address ESOL issues across the full range of government policies, and to ensure implementation across government of the CSR study recommended above.**

Case study: Coordinated regional planning

London's Strategic Action Plan for Skills for Life

Since May 2005 the Skills for Life (SfL) Flagship Group has been working with JH Consulting to develop and implement a three-year Strategic Action Plan for all ESOL in London. The overall purpose of having a joint regional Strategic Action Plan for ESOL is to establish more effective and coherent planning, purchasing and delivery of ESOL in the capital. The draft Strategic Action Plan for ESOL is available at www.jhconsulting.org.uk and a plan for literacy, numeracy and key skills is also being developed that will be released shortly. In November 2006, both plans will be formally launched. Evidence bases have been established to underpin the plans. The final draft evidence base for ESOL, which was produced in November 2005, identified the key information and issues for ESOL in London, and led to six strategic goals being agreed. These are:

- Goal 1: *To reflect and address the differing needs, characteristics and goals of 14–19 year olds and adults requiring ESOL through templates that detail how provision will be tailored.*

- Goal 2: *To ensure that people have the ESOL they need for work by delivering job-focused provision and establishing regional coordination for employment-focused ESOL.*

- Goal 3: *To target public investment on priority ESOL groups through a financing model that makes the best use of public resources, and that stimulates private sector investment.*

- Goal 4: *To ensure that promotion of ESOL learning is targeted on identified priority groups.*

- Goal 5: *To ensure consistently high quality across all ESOL provision, recognising its essential role in underpinning all curriculum provision.*

- Goal 6: *To coordinate London's Skills for Life provision through an LSC-led regional body that develops and delivers a coherent regional purchasing strategy, under the auspices of the Regional Skills Partnership.*

The evidence shows that whilst there is some really effective ESOL provision, a significant amount is not sufficiently tailored to the differing needs of learners and employers. To address this critical issue, under Goals 1 and 2, templates are being developed for each of the ESOL areas that can accommodate learners' and employers' goals, needs, learning styles and support requirements.

They are now in the process of further developing draft templates, in consultation with a wide range of stakeholders including voluntary sector partners, and matching a range of existing successful provision to the templates.

This includes 'first step' programmes and provision focused on promoting inclusion and cohesion, as well as interventions such as job brokerage or highly tailored employer provision where qualifications are not appropriate.

The templates are being used to inform a regional purchasing strategy and mechanism that will review the overall balance of public investment on ESOL against the priorities for public investment, as well as align resources from key partners. Although resources are stretched, we know that the purchasing strategy must take into account the need to prioritise groups that until now have not been able or motivated to take up learning.

A regional body has been established to take forward the further development and implementation of the Strategic Action Plan. This is not a new organisation, but represents the formalisation of relationships that have been developed between key partners, especially the LSC, London Development Agency (LDA) and Jobcentre Plus (JCP). The recently established London Strategic Unit for the Learning and Skills Workforce (LSU) will form the workforce development arm of the regional body. The LSU is currently drafting a regional SfL workforce development strategy that takes forward key elements of the Strategic Action Plan.

What is ESOL?

3.13 It may seem curious to turn to this apparently fundamental question at this point in the report. In practice the committee decided very early in its discussions that the broadest definition was the most useful: that ESOL is English language provision for adult speakers of other languages. This is a broad and inclusive working definition that embraces the fact that ESOL has to meet the needs of diverse learners who want English language for different purpose and at different levels. However, we also need to recognise that ESOL is more than just a language. The primary purpose of ESOL is English language learning, and it shares many of the features of learning other languages. The difference is that ESOL learners learn English to enable them to live and work in the UK, in other words as a tool that empowers them to gain independence and control over their lives. Language learning is necessarily about acquiring the linguistic elements of the language. However, language is more than a set of clearly defined skills, independent of the contexts in which they are used. It is inextricably linked into the different social, cultural and communicative contexts in which it is used. This means that successful communication depends on being able to recognise and know how to use language and discourse to carry out linguistic and cultural transactions. It follows from this that developing technical linguistic skills needs to be integrated with an understanding of societal institutions, structures and cultures, and how to operate and communicate within them.

3.14 We noted in our interim report that the definition of ESOL, and in particular its relationship to EFL (English as a Foreign Language) continues to have an important impact on the way in which provision is funded and, especially within further education (FE) colleges, on the way in which it is organised and managed. It is clear from the responses to our questionnaire and, indeed, from our own experience, that the distinction between ESOL and EFL, never watertight, is increasingly eroded. But the traditional distinctions do still have some important consequences in terms of funding and accreditation. ESOL provision up to and including Level 2 is currently free to learners while EFL is paid for. As a result, a number of providers have abandoned separately identified EFL provision. Where provision is mixed, this has led to classes which contain learners on different fee structures, with different learning needs and working towards different forms of accreditation. Learners have sometimes enrolled on provision which does not fully meet their learning objectives simply because it is available and free. In addition, some potential learners who would have benefited from ESOL provision have in effect been crowded out because they are more expensive to recruit and not so helpful in enabling providers to meet their targets. This has proved stressful for a number of teachers and difficult for providers to manage, particularly since they are in effect expected to enforce an increasingly complex set of entitlements and funder requirements.

3.15 It seems to us clearly inappropriate that what is now in practice an arbitrary distinction between ESOL and EFL should be relied on as one of the parameters of the funding system and have a major impact on provision. We make recommendations in section 9 about the funding system, but we believe that one of the objectives which any planning and funding arrangements for ESOL must meet is that it should enable a wide range of provision to meet the varied needs of learners with different profiles of past experience and education, different learning and study skills, different social and employment circumstances and different learning objectives. This does not happen at present.

Relationship to Skills for Life

3.16 There is a further important issue to be clarified about the nature of ESOL. In policy terms it is viewed as part of the government's wider *Skills for Life* strategy for literacy and numeracy. In many ways this is welcome: ESOL has undoubtedly benefited from the policy priority and the high profile accorded to *Skills for Life* and the resultant increase in available resource. But there are increasing concerns among policy makers and funders about the rising demand for ESOL provision which is seen as having an undue impact on the overall *Skills for Life* strategy. As we noted in paragraph 3.13, ESOL has characteristics which distinguish it from the literacy policy priority and which inevitably impact on pedagogic practice. In effect ESOL straddles the curriculum areas of *Skills for Life* and language teaching and does not align wholly with either. ESOL levels rise beyond the Level 2 ceiling of *Skills for Life*. The linguistic theories and pedagogy of foreign language teaching are almost entirely absent from *Skills for Life*, and the social inclusion and equality purposes of *Skills for Life* provision are not necessary a primary feature of foreign language provision. That consideration lay behind the recommendation in *Breaking the Language Barriers*, the first of its recommendations, that

> *All developments in the national adult basic skills strategy must address ESOL needs alongside but distinct from basic literacy and numeracy and this should be a specific responsibility of the Adult Basic Skills Strategy Unit.* (DfEE, 2000)

3.17 Much of the evidence we have considered has suggested that in practice this recommendation has not been fully addressed in the implementation of the *Skills for Life* strategy, with an adverse impact on ESOL provision that is unlikely to have been intended by policy makers. Issues include targets expressed in terms inappropriate to ESOL provision, inappropriate pedagogic requirements (including use of inappropriate formats for ILPs and pressure to teach people for the national tests without giving them the wider context which ESOL learners need) and the question of what provision can be funded. So it is now more important than ever that this recommendation is implemented. We return to a number of the relevant issues in the course of this report, but also think it appropriate to **recommend that the DfES should review the implementation of the *Skills for Life* strategy to ensure that ESOL is given appropriate attention and priority.**

The aim should be to ensure that the distinctive nature of ESOL and differences between ESOL and literacy are recognised in all aspects of implementation in order to ensure that the needs of ESOL learners are given proper attention within the overall *Skills for Life* strategy and more widely in the relevant government policies and programmes. In the funding section of this report we return to the question of which elements of ESOL should continue to qualify for the funding available for *Skills for Life* learners, and which should be treated differently in funding terms. But we are clear that the essential link between *Skills for Life* and ESOL should not be broken.

3.18 The relationship with adult literacy is very complex but it is an important concern when considering the relationship of ESOL to *Skills for Life*. The key issues relate to meeting the reading and writing learning needs of ESOL learners. These can be complex and are not always recognised or addressed either in ESOL or adult literacy programmes. Learners range from those with very little experience of reading and writing in their first language to those with highly sophisticated literacy skills in one or more other languages. Their language profiles also differ so that oracy skills can be more developed than reading and writing skills, or vice versa. It is difficult to meet these needs in generic provision. Learners who have little experience of reading and writing in any language often need specialist support to enable them to learn and progress. When they are placed in classes where this is not available they can fail to thrive, become demotivated or drop out. Adults with well-developed oracy but less experience of other literacy skills can find the speaking and listening content of generic ESOL classes at their literacy threshold too basic and undemanding, but struggle in higher-level courses where the literacy demands are too great.

3.19   Although the numbers are difficult to quantify, we know that some bilingual and multilingual adults learn in adult literacy classes. They might choose to do so because they do not identify as ESOL learners, because they want to learn alongside English speakers or they feel comfortable with their oral skills and want to focus on other literacy skills. Some have no alternative since ESOL is not offered, as is often the case in rural areas or community venues in neighbourhoods where there are insufficient numbers of adults wanting ESOL classes to make courses economically viable. They might benefit from the opportunity to interact with English speakers. However, their specific language skills development needs are often different from those of native speakers of English, and there can be a detrimental effect on learning where teachers are not equipped with the specialist knowledge to respond.

3.20   It is clear that teachers need training to equip them with the skills to manage ESOL written literacy learning, which is not yet a widespread feature of ESOL training, although this will change in the new qualifications. There are also implications for the organisation of provision. For example, should learners develop literacy skills in specific reading and writing programmes? Some teachers have suggested that it is particularly difficult to develop reading and writing skills in the group environment, especially in mixed level classes, and these learners might benefit from supplementary individual tuition although this is very resource intensive. As there has been little research into teaching literacy to bilingual adults in the UK (Barton and Pitt, 2003; Spiegel and Sunderland, 2006), our knowledge about the distinctive features of ESOL written literacy acquisition, the influence of first languages, and the most effective pedagogical approaches is still underdeveloped, and it is not possible to designate any particular approach as 'correct'. What is important is that teachers are trained and confident with literacy pedagogy and are able to stretch learners to enable them to extract maximum benefit from reading and writing learning approaches and materials.

3.21   One current initiative where the link between the two areas will be particularly important is the development of functional skills: it is essential that the specific issues related to ESOL are considered in this development work. The point is not that different standards are required for ESOL, but that distinctive guidance on pedagogy and delivery is required for the application of the standards in the very different contexts in which ESOL learning takes place.

In order to address this and other issues more effectively **we recommend that the DfES should convene a national advisory group or forum on ESOL to act as a source of expertise and advice on ESOL issues and to ensure that policy developments across government take full account of ESOL issues.**

We note that it is the intention of the Scottish Executive to establish such a forum and think that connections could helpfully be established between the two bodies.

Who are the learners?

3.22   We have noted already at several points in this report that the profile of ESOL learners has been changing. In 2000, *Breaking the Language Barriers* identified four broad categories of learner:
- Settled communities
- Refugees and asylum seekers
- Migrant workers
- Partners and spouses of learners.

3.23 It recognised that within these broad groups, the needs, aspirations and educational backgrounds of learners varied widely. It is clear that these four groups remain the core client groups. But there has been a marked increase in the number of learners from the EU, specifically migrant workers from the A8 countries. This has had a number of important consequences for demand and an impact on the nature of provision. Learner cohorts have become even more heterogeneous, with diverse priorities, expectations, educational and cultural backgrounds and different legal status. Many migrant workers need provision specifically geared to their work situation; language skills appropriate to the demands and needs of their work, including communication and workplace cultures. It should include issues which confront them living in their communities, offer potential progression opportunities, and be available at times to fit with working hours. There are now demands for ESOL in areas of England which have little or no tradition of making such provision, for example in rural areas with concentrations of A8 migrant agricultural workers. This presents a significant challenge to the current infrastructure. However, it is difficult to be precise about the extent of A8 learner demand. The most recent (2004–5) LSC figures suggest that such learners remain only a small proportion of total ESOL enrolments – some 4.03 per cent. This is almost certainly a significant underestimate as the Individual Learner Record (ILR) information only asks for country of residence and there are implausibly large numbers of white British learners enrolled on ESOL. But that even these figures mask a sharp increase is shown by the fact that enrolments by Polish nationals increased from 151 in 2000–1 to 21,313 in 2004–5. Respondents to our questionnaire suggest that these figures substantially understate the current scale of demand, that it increased sharply in 2005–6, and continues to grow. It is regrettable that up-to-date and reliable enrolment figures are not available from the LSC, although we recognise the difficulty in providing them.

Learner profile: The Aktas family

Mursel is a 39-year-old Turkish man who works long hours in a kebab shop. Ali, his son, and Leyla, 18, his daughter, work at local factories. Despite all this, all three are committed to the English for Speakers of Other Languages programme and never miss a lesson. The family's determination to achieve through learning is already reaping rewards for them as Ali recently attained a first class Pitman Basic English qualification.

3.24 Some particular issues arise in relation to migrant workers (EU and non-EU). They are open to exploitation by unscrupulous employers: the Trades Union Congress (TUC) has described the legal protection available to such workers as 'wholly inadequate' (TUC, 2003) and such vulnerability is clearly increased if workers do not possess adequate English language skills and therefore find it difficult to acquire knowledge of or access to the systems which might protect them. In some parts of the country, the families of migrant workers are increasingly joining them: although the level of demand from these adults for ESOL provision is not known, it clearly has implications for the planning of provision in the relevant areas, many of them already under pressure to meet the demands of the migrant workers themselves.

3.25 This increasing demand raises the question of how EU migrant workers' ESOL needs should be paid for, and whether they and/or their employers should bear some proportion of the cost. We believe that there is a strong case that employers who benefit from the recruitment of migrant workers should have a responsibility to ensure that their workers have adequate language skills for the purposes of their work and their period of time as members of the community in England. We are encouraged by the declared intention of the Confederation of British Industry (CBI) to work with its members to 'encourage the provision of English language training to those who need it'.[6]

---

6 http://www.employabilityforum.co.uk/documents/CBI-TUC-Home_Office_Joint-Statement.pdf

We recommend that the new criteria for the designation of A-rated sponsors for non-EU migrant workers should include the provision of appropriate ESOL training.

Learner profile: Pjotr

Pjotr is 22 years old and from Estonia. He arrived in England in 2004, is an EU citizen and is currently unemployed. Pjotr was a forklift truck driver in Estonia and is hoping to gain similar employment in the UK. He joined English classes to improve his chances of employment, and needed to focus on applications and interviews. When asked where he had acquired his English skills he said he could remember a small amount from school and had taught himself since he came to England. He has made fast progress and has commented that the classes give him confidence to speak in many new situations outside the classroom.

3.26 Alongside these relatively new needs, there remains significant demand from the more traditional learner groups. Approximately 90 per cent of LSC-funded provision relates to residents of England or 'home learners.' This figure will include learners from elsewhere in the EU, including the A8 countries. Many settled residents want to improve their English many years after arrival; perhaps because they have had little space in busy working lives to attend classes, have relied on family or community support, or have been unaware of or reluctant to access learning opportunities, or been discouraged by the lack of accessible provision or support such as childcare. New naturalisation requirements mean that many settled residents now also have a requirement to learn English. Characteristically these potential learners find difficulties accessing provision, requiring outreach work to make initial contact and often prefer targeted home or community-based provision, which is expensive and time-consuming to provide. There is a real danger that when there are full classes and long waiting lists of potential learners who are easier to reach and to teach, these groups will be excluded. There is also the risk that some members of the resident communities who have had few educational opportunities and may have no or limited written literacy skills (particularly women) become reluctant to join classes where provision designed to meet their specific needs is not available. Learning alongside more recent arrivals with higher-level literacy and study skills can be a major deterrent.

3.27 There are still substantial numbers of migrants joining settled communities usually for family migration where spouses or fiancées and/or children join their families, the majority of them women from regions outside Europe. This means that they are not able to benefit from state-funded learning provision until one year after arrival. Yet there is evidence to suggest that their need to acquire language skills to enable them to settle and integrate effectively is most acute early on, and that the longer a learner has been in the UK the less likely they are to be making progress. It will therefore be all the harder for them to learn effectively if they have to wait for access to provision (Baynham *et al.*, forthcoming).

3.28 There are particular issues in relation to refugees and asylum seekers.[7] The government's policy of dispersing asylum seekers across the UK has led to particular pressures for service providers in cities and towns with little or no experience of providing services for asylum seekers. ESOL providers in these circumstances have had to adapt to learners with whose background they are unfamiliar and who suffer from multiple problems which affect their learning. Learners will often look to their ESOL teachers to help them with these wider issues, and not all teachers will be equipped to help learners in this way, nor should they be expected to. The range of learners in this category is particularly wide: often asylum seekers are highly resourceful, skilled and resilient people[8] with the capacity to contribute a great deal to

---

[7] We use the following definitions. A *refugee* is someone who has fled, or is unable to return to, their country of origin because of a 'well-founded fear of persecution due to race, religion, nationality, political opinion or membership of a social group'. A person becomes a refugee by claiming asylum and having that claim approved. An *asylum seeker* is a person who has claimed refugee status and is waiting for a decision on that claim.

[8] A Home Office survey in 2004 found that most refugees were working or students before they left their country of origin, over 40 per cent held qualifications and around 75 per cent could read and write some English.

UK society. But asylum seekers do not have the right to work until a decision is made on their status, and there have often been long waits before a decision is taken. Many practitioners are of the view that asylum seekers need full-time provision for both language skills and employability if they are to make progress. Such provision would prepare those asylum seekers whose applications are successful, but would also benefit those many applicants who have to wait for very long periods for decisions and have a real impact on social cohesion in the areas in which they live. But it is impossible to make such provision because of the need to meet a high and increasing level of demand within limited resources. It is also difficult to draw down funding for work experience, which is a key element in successful provision and some asylum seekers have been denied permission even to undertake unpaid work experience.

3.29 Refugees are often out of work or employed in work below their capability and qualifications. Current financial support arrangements make it difficult for them to undertake full-time employability training or voluntary work which would help them obtain work at a level which would enable them to make their full potential contribution to UK society. Jobseeker's Allowance regulations require refugees to take any available work: what is on offer is often not commensurate with the level of their skills and qualifications. Once in this work they have little time to pursue the English studies that would enable them to secure more appropriate, usually better-paid and more productive work.

Learner profile: Siboneleni Nkomo

Siboneleni said that, 'attending this course dramatically changed my life', and gave her the confidence to apply for a part-time job as a carer, which has enabled to her to realise her goal of not relying on state benefits.

A proud woman who was a homeowner with a business in her own country, Siboneleni had to flee her home, arriving in the UK traumatised and with a young family. She experienced problems with language, episodes of racism and increasing isolation, yet throughout this time her overriding ambition has been to become a fully integrated part of the local community and get away from the culture of dependency she experienced when she first arrived in the UK.

She never gave up and her dedication and pursuit of independence is inspiring. She enrolled on a storytelling project, and even had her story aired on local radio. She has found the confidence to make friends and get work. She now supports a woman with epilepsy as well as continuing to study.

3.30 Respondents to our questionnaire, in particular from colleges, report that there are increasing numbers of young learners who need ESOL provision. As well as unaccompanied minors seeking asylum, many adolescents arrive to join their families, especially from the Indian subcontinent. Some 14–16 year olds cannot secure places in school, many in year 11 where schools are focused on GCSE attainment. Some of these young learners need full-time and holiday support, and have emotional and behavioural development needs in addition to their language and cultural learning requirements. Colleges face increasing demand to accommodate these young learners, are not resourced to meet all their needs, and are not able to access the resources which are available to the school system to support these learners.

> ## Learner profile: Kenadid
>
> *Kenadid arrived with a group of unaccompanied minors. He joined a step into science course but suffered from depression and culture shock, homesickness and the continuing lack of any news about the whereabouts of his remaining family. This was aggravated by money issues. Kenadid was prescribed antidepressants, which made him very tired and affected his studies. His appearance had also deteriorated as he had no new clothing since his arrival. Teachers and college support services arranged support with his finances, a donation of clothing and partnered him with a buddy on the same course. He is now settled in college and making progress in his studies.*

3.31 There are some other specific areas of demand to which respondents to our consultation have drawn attention:

- Some migrant workers want short courses giving basic language skills, and are not interested in the courses attracting accreditation which are the priority for LSC funding. Some employers similarly want short English for work courses and are not interested in their employees getting any accreditation.
- There is evidence of demand for international English and IELTS[9] courses: many learners cannot afford these but need them if they are to make their full potential contribution to the labour market.
- The LSC's funding priorities and differing local interpretations of their implications also make it hard to meet the demand for Pre-Entry level and Entry Levels 1 and 2 learning.

There is still insufficient workplace and embedded[10] provision (an issue which goes wider than ESOL, and one to which we return below).

3.32 It is, as always, difficult to quantify unmet demand precisely, and we must be careful not to give undue weight to anecdotal evidence. But the consistency of the responses to our questionnaire, and evidence from a range of other sources, suggests that there are important issues to be addressed. This is not simply a matter of increasing funding: there are also important questions about the nature of provision and its delivery which we address below. At the least, we must raise the question of whether the available resource is being used as effectively as possible, and in a way which is equitable between groups of learners, meets the needs of the most disadvantaged, takes into account ability to pay and benefits the economy. There is a disturbing amount of evidence that this is not currently the case and our proposals on funding in section 9 are intended to help address this key issue.

---

9   IELTS (International English Language Testing System) is the qualification required for health and other professions where eligibility to work is conditional on gaining a high IELTS score. It is also used for access to degree and other professional courses at many HEIs.

10 The term 'embedded learning' has been adopted over the past few years to describe approaches to developing language (and literacy and numeracy) skills within and as an integral element of another learning programme.

4

ESOL and social inclusion

This section sets out the many ways in which ESOL is relevant to social inclusion and argues that it is essential that the new Commission on Integration and Cohesion takes full account of language issues. We discuss the importance of ESOL to citizenship and recommend that its impact on current policies on children and the 14–19 group should be reviewed. We argue for an increase in the resources devoted to ESOL in family learning and for a planned and managed approach to improving ESOL for offenders.

4.1 In section 3 we noted that the relevance of language skills to policy on citizenship has been explicitly acknowledged and acted upon. But the relevance of language skills, and ESOL in particular, to issues of social justice and inclusion goes much wider than the formal requirements of citizenship, important though these are. The government's vision of a 'strong and fair society' is very relevant to ESOL learners.

> *The test of a strong and fair society is whether the most vulnerable can thrive. Thriving in modern Britain means more than 'just getting by' – it means living a life with prospects, dignity and a sense of control. That is our aspiration for everyone and we have helped many people to achieve it – e.g. by raising educational standards, lowering pensioner poverty and reducing fear of crime but it is not yet a reality for many of our most disadvantaged citizens.* (ODPM, 2005)

For many, improving their language skills will be a vital early step on the road to being able to thrive in British society in the ways the government desires for all citizens. We have already noted that language skills are essential to enable people to get jobs, get access to public services and make informed choices about them, understand their rights and responsibilities and participate as citizens in the life of their communities and nation.

4.2 It is well documented that people from black and minority ethnic communities are disproportionately at risk of living in disadvantaged areas, being unemployed and suffering from poor health. The same is true for most asylum seekers and refugees. The challenges facing these groups are often compounded where they lack language skills. Many of these problems are also experienced by relatively well-paid migrant workers. ESOL provision has a key role in enabling these groups to thrive in the UK.

4.3 Gender is a further significant consideration. Women often experience additional discrimination, and have particular difficulties that are often overlooked (Home Office, 2001; Refugee Council, 2005a). Gender or cultural factors can affect aspirations or restrict opportunities to attend classes, for instance lack of crèche places or locally accessible learning opportunities particularly affects women as they are the primary group of carers. In some groups women's language skills are less well developed than those of men. Only 4 per cent of Bangladeshi women and 28 per cent of Pakistani women have good or fluent English, for example (Tackey *et al.*, 2006), and a recent study found that 63 per cent of male asylum seekers claimed to be proficient in written and spoken English whilst most women asserted they had limited understanding of written and/or spoken English (Dumper, 2002; Kirk, 2004; Refugee Council, 2005b). Many women are disadvantaged in the labour market, and the participation rates of Pakistani and Bangladeshi women are especially low. Women asylum seekers and refugees face particular challenges. If they arrive with a partner, the man is usually deemed the principal applicant, and as a result the woman has relatively little autonomy. Women living alone or with children, more than ever if they lack language skills, have restricted access to health and other support services. Many live in fear for their safety, and some endure domestic violence (Dumper, 2002; Kofman *et al.*, 2005; Refugee Council, 2005a). All these factors mean that different strategies are needed to ensure that all women have opportunities to access English language provision. We have heard from providers, often local authorities, who seek to prioritise excluded women. We have also heard about providers who see little incentive to invest in outreach work to engage older Somali women or young Bangladeshi mothers, for instance, when they already have bulging classes, with more on long waiting lists. When this happens sections of the population are excluded, often women whose lives might be significantly enhanced by the opportunities and wider horizons they could gain through attending English language provision.

4.4   Family migration enables spouses, fiancés and fiancées to join settled communities. It is highly feminised, with significantly more wives and fiancées entering than husbands and fiancés, almost all from outside the EU (Kofman *et al.*, 2005). This means that they are not eligible for free state-funded learning provision for three years, or one year for those eligible under the spouses residency rule. This rule disbars bilingual adults, usually women, from free provision at the time when they need to learn as quickly as possible to support them to settle. It is so much harder, for example, for young women to find work of the same status or go through their first pregnancy in an unfamiliar health environment without the language and cultural knowledge they need to help them. As their ability to communicate is severely constrained, they remain, 'submerged in their own communities and may already have suffered permanent communication problems with mainstream society' (Crick, 2006). The negative impacts can be compounded when they are able to start learning, as research indicates that delays in starting to learn English have a detrimental effect on ability to learn and progress (Baynham *et al.*, forthcoming).

4.5   It is important also to note the key social role that ESOL provision itself plays for many learners. The ESOL class can become a stabilising element in what are often difficult, even chaotic, lives. For many learners their class will be a rare opportunity to socialise with others with similar issues, and the mutual support which learners can give to each other can be immensely valuable. ESOL classes are often important for the cohesion of the communities from which learners are drawn. The teachers and support workers of ESOL classes are usually very committed to their learners, and give them support which goes well beyond the acquisition of language skills, offering them support, advice, links to other services and advocacy. This raises important issues about the skills required by those working in ESOL and we return to this issue in section 6.

4.6   The impact of provision on the social inclusion of ESOL learners can, of course, go well beyond being a by-product of conventional language classes. Programmes can be designed to weave together language skills and material which is designed to empower learners to take active roles in their communities as well as to address the wider issues which confront them. Devising such programmes presents real challenges in terms of curriculum, content and pedagogy and this is an area which, with the exception of the materials on citizenship that we have already noted, is underdeveloped. There are three specific areas we look at in more detail: citizenship, family learning and community involvement. We also look at ESOL for offenders. In each of these areas, ESOL potentially has a vital role to play.

Citizenship

4.7   We think that the link in current policy between citizenship and language skills is right. The language requirement for citizenship is that if applicants do not have language skills (in English, Welsh or Scottish Gaelic) at Entry Level 3 or above, they must successfully complete a citizenship and language skills course. This is a language course which uses learning materials incorporating information about life in the UK. Learners do not have to reach Entry Level 3 to satisfy requirements for citizenship; they need only to progress one level. It is, of course, essential for the success of this policy that there is adequate provision to enable people to acquire the skills they need to meet these requirements. Relevant learning materials are one aspect of this, and we welcome the materials commissioned by the Home Office and DfES and devised by NIACE and LLU+ at London South Bank University which have been successfully introduced in practice in England. We hope that they will be disseminated and used more widely. It is clearly important that such dissemination includes training of ESOL teachers to use the materials effectively. We are pleased to note that other countries in the UK are developing their own materials along similar lines.

4.8 We understand that it is likely that competence in English language will be introduced as a new criterion for settlement for non-EU migrants, on the same lines as the language criteria for citizenship and likely to be tested in a similar way. We are not clear whether any firm estimate has been made of the numbers of people likely to want to access English language provision to develop the skills they need to qualify for settlement: we recognise that such an estimate is not likely to be easy to make. But it is clearly important to arrive at the best estimate possible of the likely additional pressures on ESOL provision, to make provision to meet them and to be clear about the funding arrangements which apply.

4.9 However, the issue of ESOL and citizenship goes wider than the instrumental link with the formal requirements of citizenship and settlement. The requirement that applicants for citizenship acquire English language skills is clearly intended to assist their integration into UK society, as part of wider efforts to build cohesive communities. Recently, there have been calls from government for a debate on the value of multiculturalism, questioning whether earlier policy objectives have encouraged separateness.[11] We would encourage continuation of valuing and celebrating diversity and difference. It is welcome that the NIACE/LLU+ materials mentioned above are seen as enabling users to connect with British society, systems and cultures while valuing their own backgrounds. In developing ESOL policy it is important that it should not be used to deny the value of learners' backgrounds and cultural heritages.

ESOL and family learning

4.10 Many ESOL learners are parents or carers, and current policy and practice emphasises the importance of parental involvement in children's learning and, increasingly, in participating in shaping and planning activities in childcare organisations and schools (DfES, 2005a; HM Government, 2004). Parents' and carers' language skills can affect how well they relate to and influence childcare and education providers, as well as being important in enabling them to support their children's care and education. Ofsted has identified language support needs amongst second generation children from bilingual families as a key issue (Ofsted, 2005). Family learning provision can make a powerful contribution to children's educational achievement as well as bringing benefits to whole families and the schools in which their children learn (DfES, 2005a). It provides opportunities for parents to develop their own language skills as well as their ability to help to raise their children's education achievements and aspirations. This is important because a proportion of the large numbers of children from black and minority ethnic families who fail to reach their full potential at school will be from bilingual families (Home Office, 2005a).

4.11 It is therefore important that the childcare workforce recruitment strategy in this area should include bilingual and multilingual staff to ensure that it reflects the cultural plurality of society and enriches the experiences and outlooks that services offer to children. Such workers can also provide valuable bridges and cultural translations between childcare organisations, schools and homes. ESOL provision can offer development opportunities to equip adults from minority communities to secure employment in this important sector.

---

[11] Ruth Kelly, text of speech available: http://www.communities.gov.uk/index.asp?id=1502280

4.12 Many schools have developed in-depth understanding of their pupils' cultures and their parents' views on education, responding in ways that respect diverse cultures whilst developing parents' confidence to participate in school life and support their children's learning.

> *'I learnt more ideas from my other friends here (the family learning class) about how they treat their children, how they play with their children, and it made me learn about the education system in Britain, which every mother needs to know, because it's much different from the education system in Iraq. Even the way they are teaching children here is very different.'*
> *(Sawsan)* (Rees et al., 2003)

In other schools, misunderstandings arise between school staff and bilingual parents and carers, often stemming from contradictory cultural expectations of the function of schools and roles of parents in education processes (Gregory, 1996). Bilingual parents tend to recognise their lack of knowledge of the British education system for instance, but at the same time have extremely high aspirations for their children, and often feel that schools have low expectations and do not stretch their children enough. This can be particularly acute where the teaching methods used are very different to those employed in their own educational culture. On the other hand schools expect high levels of parental involvement in supporting children with their learning, and can be frustrated where parents fail to do so, often not realising that these parents regard academic development as the school's responsibility and their role as nurturing and caring. Lack of English language skills can also inhibit some parents.

4.13 However, research has indicated that these same parents are often highly active in pursuing their children's development of first languages, and that changes in school practice which recognise and develop bilingual parents' capacity to help their children can accelerate progress (Gregory, 1996). Family learning provision can be an enormous help in enabling teachers, parents and carers to negotiate these cultural boundaries, and this can be particularly useful to schools with little or no experience of this type of issue striving to work with new communities of refugees, asylum seekers and migrant workers. ESOL family learning is often provided through the national Skills for Families programme, funded through the LSC. These programmes aim to develop parents' language skills, enhance their ability to help their children and boost their children's language acquisition. They are also an important access point to learning for women, as, despite cultural shifts in relation to gender, caring is still predominantly women's responsibility. We return to this issue in section 9.25.

> *'After my husband died I didn't know anyone in England. Before the family learning course I found English hard but in the class I talked to other parents. I met lots of parents and even teachers and now I know lots of people and I have friends. Now my daughter always does well in class and gets an award at the end of the year. After my husband died my son was difficult but after going to school now he is OK, he also does well in class....*
>
> *I also speak a lot of English now. The courses changed my life one hundred per cent. Now I can go out. I have friends and I can study.'* (Ruby) (Rees et al., 2003)

The guidance also stresses the importance of celebrating cultural practices and using first languages to support learning (DfES, 2005a).

> *'I joined the course and now I understand more about bilingualism and I'm more confident about myself and how to bring up my children in this country.'* (Sawsan) (Rees et al., 2003)

4.14 Support for children and families, especially those living in poor areas, includes Sure Start Children's Centres which support disadvantaged families with young children. One challenge they face is to ensure that children from black and minority ethnic families benefit, and this has particular application for ESOL learners since bilingual and multilingual parents are often unaware of services or the benefits they can offer, and sometimes experience inappropriate provision. We have noted elsewhere the important role that ESOL teachers often play in making ESOL learners aware of the services available to them, and it is important that Sure Start Children's Centres should be aware of this potential support and develop links with relevant ESOL providers.

4.15   Extended Schools are being introduced under the *Every Child Matters* policy to offer a wide range of services to children and their parents in the community they serve during an extended school day. These services will include childcare, parenting and adult learning programmes, health and social care support services, and after school activities, and a fundamental principle of their development is consulting with parents and involving them in planning services (DfES, 2005d). Ensuring that bilingual families are active in these processes will enrich whole school communities, and at the same time help them to accord value to all the cultures and languages of their communities. A great deal of good practice has been developed in ESOL family learning and this can be built on to help learners acquire the skills they need to take an active part in transactions such as consultative arrangements and to influence the ethos and organisational aspects of school and childcare provision.

4.16   We believe that there is clearly scope for greater synergy between the areas of work to take forward *Every Child Matters* and the 14–19 strategy and ESOL provision.

We recommend that DfES should ensure that the links with ESOL policy, provision and providers have been effectively made in relation to each of the key aspects of the implementation of *Every Child Matters* and the 14–19 strategy.

ESOL and community involvement

4.17   Language skills are the essential underpinning of wider involvement in the community, whether at local or national level, in the work environment or in neighbourhoods. They are required to enable people to participate in democratic structures and to take leadership roles in the community, and thus to help build community capacity, an important element of policy on community regeneration. It is important to note that many of those with language needs are skilled and resourceful people who have survived adversity and have the qualities to play significant roles in their new communities, although there are some (particularly amongst those who are seeking asylum) who were politically active in their countries of origin and will wish to avoid activities which may jeopardise their safety in the UK.

Case study: Developing skills and language support for community participation

Bolton Community College's Learning Ambassadors Project has provided a very effective progression route for second language learners. Originally designed as a scheme for recruiting and training local learning mentors, the project has developed beyond this into one that equips participants with the skills to research into the needs of communities and to support individuals/groups in a variety of ways. The project has attracted commissions from a range of agencies to undertake research on their behalf and has been able to provide paid work experience for trained ambassadors. The project has utilised the bilingual skills/expertise of many second language learners in this work. The project therefore has enabled second language learners to improve their language skills, develop confidence, acquire relevant qualifications, and gain valuable work experience, and many have progressed onto higher-level training and/or employment.

4.18 This issue is of particular significance in the light of current policy on ensuring a greater role for citizens in shaping local services (following the Lyons report (2006)) and is clearly also relevant to the work of the Commission on Integration and Cohesion announced by Ruth Kelly, the Secretary of State for Communities and Local Government in August 2006. Ruth Kelly's speech at the launch of the Commission referred to encouraging local authorities and community organisations to increase the availability of English language teaching.[12] We warmly welcome this initiative. It is essential that the Commission takes full account of the importance of language issues to wider issues of integration and cohesion, and that it plays a role in securing the greater coherence of government policy in this area for which we have argued earlier in this report. We recognise, of course, that language skills are, of course, only one element in regeneration, social and democratic participation, but they are an important element, and it is vital that policy development on these issues should take account of the language dimension, as should the work of the agencies on the ground responsible for policy implementation.

We recommend that the DfES and appropriate partners should commission a national programme to develop, test and disseminate models and materials for ESOL to support community and democratic participation.

ESOL for offenders

4.19 Offenders from black and ethnic minority communities comprise 19 per cent of the male and 25 per cent of the female prison population compared to approximately 7.5 per cent of the general population of England and Wales.[13] Although precise figures are not available, a proportion of these are bilingual and multilingual adults with English language development needs. The length of their stay, background, education and employment histories and language competence are very varied (Dalziel and Sofres, 2005).

4.20 The importance of learning in supporting offenders into sustainable employment, playing a positive role in their communities and reducing re-offending through developing literacy, language, numeracy and vocational skills and qualifications is widely recognised (see, for instance, DfES, 2005c; cf. also Home Office, 2006). In addition, all offenders, even those likely to be deported at the end of their sentence, need language skills to enable them to remain safe within the prison environment, and to cooperate fully with the authorities while serving their sentence. In spite of this, offenders face significant barriers to accessing education, training and employment, and these are more acute for those with English language development needs.[14] These obstacles are inherent in the current system. Whilst there are some very committed teachers and creative and inspiring teaching (Dalziel and Sofres, 2005), there are also serious concerns about poor quality of provision where learners experience inadequate assessments of need and monitoring of progress, and are offered uninspired teaching supported by inappropriate materials. Where there are small numbers of ESOL learners in individual custodial settings, they are in literacy or mixed level ESOL classes that do not fully meet their needs. Offenders serving sentences in the community often find provision difficult to access (ALI, 2004a; Dalziel and Sofres, 2005; Ward and Kerwin, 2005)[15] Furthermore, both teachers' and learners' efforts are frequently undermined by prison regimes. Learning in custody is regularly disrupted as sessions are cancelled or learners are transferred to different institutions. Learning is paid at a lower rate than work so that inmates have to choose between learning and making money. In some institutions classes coincide with shower times presenting another sort of choice, and prison officers' attitudes to learning range from positive to hostile (ALI, 2004b; Braggins and Talbot, 2003; Dalziel and Sofres, 2005; Uden, 2004).[16] The 2002 ESOL Prison Pathfinders report concluded that there would be substantial benefits in upgrading ESOL in prisons (Dalziel and Sofres, 2005).

---

[12] Ruth Kelly, text of speech available: http://www.communities.gov.uk/index.asp?id=1502280
[13] Source: Prison statistics, England and Wales, 2002 quoted www.dfes.gov.uk/offenderlearning
[14] DfES Offenders Learning and Skills Unit.
[15] See also Home Office Detention Centre inspection reports, Ofsted/ALI.
[16] See also Home Office Detention Centre inspection reports, Ofsted/ALI.

4.21 The problematic aspects of learning provision for offenders are being tackled by a radical change in the way that all offender learning and skills provision is planned, funded and delivered. The LSC has assumed responsibility for planning and funding all learning and skills provision for offenders and will work in close partnership with the National Offender Management Service, National Probation Service and other partners to bring more coherence to offender education and training across custody and community settings. Offenders' access to ESOL is to be enhanced through interventions that include staff training, improving initial assessment processes and ensuring cohesive learning journeys as they serve their sentences. A green paper was published in December 2005 setting out the government's strategy to help reduce re-offending by improving skills and employment opportunities for offenders (DfES, 2005b). These are all welcome developments but **we recommend that the planned improvements to ESOL for offenders in custodial and community settings should be pursued actively in a planned and monitored programme if the current deplorable state of ESOL for offenders is to be remedied.**

5

ESOL and work

Many ESOL learners are motivated by the wish to find work. Often they cannot get access to appropriate provision and there has been too little progress in developing work-related ESOL provision. We are concerned that the resources available in this area may have been reduced following the recent transfer of responsibility for employability training to the LSC and think it essential to keep a focus on learning as well as employment outcomes in the new programme which is being developed. Work is needed to develop appropriate models for workplace-based provision and to encourage employers to adopt them.

The current position

5.1   Many ESOL learners are motivated by the need to find work or to improve their position in the labour market. Employment is one of the key factors in successful integration: it provides economic independence, enhances self-esteem, provides a recognised place in society and provides opportunities to practise and improve language skills. As we have noted above, ESOL can also make an important contribution to overall economic prosperity, as migrants will be increasingly important to the UK labour market in the medium term. But there is worrying evidence that current ESOL provision is not well adapted to helping people with English language needs, whether migrants or members of the settled population, to work to their full potential and to contribute as well as they could to the economy.

5.2   There are important differences between the levels of participation in the labour market between different groups of people with English language needs:

- Asylum seekers are not allowed to work while their case is under review.
- Migrant workers from the A8 countries have high rates of employment, but often in unskilled and poorly-paid work.
- Fewer than half the working age adults of Pakistani and Bangladeshi origin are in work.
- Women's participation rates are lower than those of men.
- Many migrants with high-level qualifications and skills find it very difficult to get employment which fully uses their skills and experience.
- Benefit rules can make it difficult for unemployed adults to access full-time vocational and employability provision with language support.

5.3   The responses to our consultation have indicated significant barriers which inhibit people from accessing effective work-related provision:

- Lack of awareness of available provision, often the result of the lack of specialist information, advice and guidance.
- Jobcentres are not resourced to adequately identify the ESOL needs of migrants, particularly those with higher or professional level skills.
- In some areas there is a shortage of ESOL tutors and funding.

- Providers are sometimes reluctant or unable to make provision which addresses employment issues as well as language skills, and links between employers and providers of vocational training are often not effective.
- Tutors are often not trained or experienced in providing workplace-based learning.
- It is often difficult for people in work to access provision because it is not offered in working hours, or does not fit with shift patterns, or people's working hours are very long.
- There is often a lack of suitable work placements which are vital to reinforce language skills in an employment setting.
- Many migrant workers are highly mobile, following work opportunities to different areas of the country which makes it difficult to establish a consistent and progressive pattern of learning.

5.4 Lack of effective English language skills is an important obstacle for many people in getting into the labour market or progressing within it. But it is not the only factor, and it is important to be aware of some of the other relevant barriers in thinking about how ESOL provision can help address these issues.

- There is a worrying level of public hostility to migrants and members of minority ethnic communities. For example, concern is expressed that migrants drive down pay and worsen working conditions. Research indicates that there is virtually no evidence that this is happening at present (Gilpin *et al.*, 2006), although this is clearly an important issue to continue to monitor.
- Some employers are reluctant to employ people in these groups because they do not fully understand the rules about refugee and asylum seeker status and fear prosecution if they employ someone who is not entitled to work.
- Refugees have to seek employment as soon as their status is confirmed and this can lead to their being trapped in low-paid employment below their levels of skills and experience. The same can be true of long-term settled migrants.
- People often have difficulty in producing evidence of their qualifications gained overseas and/or in gaining recognition of such qualifications.
- Gaining higher-level qualifications to prove English language competence, for example through the IELTS, is expensive and difficult even where provision is available, as it is not in all areas of the country.
- Lack of English language skills is often accompanied by limited awareness of the culture of employment in the UK, with different patterns and avenues of recruitment as well as different work practices.

5.5 Effective work-focused ESOL provision has to address some of these wider matters, in particular issues of acculturation. Work-focused provision is required both for those not currently in work, focusing on employability, and workplace-based ESOL for those already in work, to improve their skills and productivity in their current roles and to give them a base from which they can progress in the labour market. But it is clear that most English language provision is not work focused: it is general provision, at lower levels, in effect survival English. There is little work-focused ESOL provision, and even less focused on specific occupations.

5.6 It is important to note that there are examples of excellent practice in the provision of work-related ESOL, and it is essential that we should learn from these. But there is a wider need to develop a strategy for work-focused provision, a pedagogic approach which incorporates the lessons from the most effective current practice, and funding arrangements which do not militate against such provision.

Possible approaches

Vocational ESOL

5.7 It is clear that integrating ESOL with the teaching of vocational skills is an effective approach to the needs of learners seeking work, but it is an area which is still underdeveloped. This must be a particular worry given the increasing demands for skills at Levels 2 and 3 identified by the Leitch review. One area of particular concern in the inspectorate reports is the lack of progress in effectively embedding ESOL in vocational curriculum areas. This also applies to literacy and numeracy. The pedagogic implications of embedding are not yet fully explored, but it is clear that many teachers of vocational subjects are neither trained nor confident in dealing with the ESOL needs of their learners. In addition, many are not fully aware of the likely needs and how they can most effectively be addressed. It is welcome that the DfES has commissioned Lifelong Learning UK (LLUK) to develop new routes for vocational teachers to ensure that they have the skills required to ensure that basic skills and ESOL elements can be embedded into vocational courses. Research (Roberts *et al.*, 2005) indicates that the most effective means of ensuring that language needs are effectively addressed is the involvement of a specialist language teacher in supporting design and delivery of language support, although there are different models for putting this into place. All of these models incur additional costs and require effective management through a whole-organisation approach with a clear sense of direction, and appropriate support for professional development, supported by senior management.

Case study: Embedded vocational provision

ESOL Plus Childcare is a very popular and highly successful vocational ESOL programme offered within the School of ESOL at Waltham Forest College. The course runs over a 36-week academic year. Learners have 7.5 hours of Childcare a week leading to the CACHE Foundation Award in Caring for Children. Learners have a further eight hours of ESOL a week which supports them in their Childcare study and also prepares them to take ESOL Skills for Life exams. There is very close cooperation and coordination between staff in the Childcare and ESOL areas to ensure that the English classes particularly develop the language and study skills learners need to complete their current and future Childcare studies and to work as a professional in that area. The success of the programme is evidenced by the fact that a high proportion of learners achieve both in Childcare, often gaining distinctions, and in ESOL, and that every year a significant number of learners progress to Level 2 Childcare courses. In the present year we have introduced a second, lower-level ESOL Plus Childcare programme which incorporates the CACHE Entry Level Certificate in Preparation for Childcare. This is designed to enable ESOL learners with insufficient language skills to take the Foundation Award nevertheless to embark on supported Childcare study.

Waltham Forest College

5.8   Some providers in responding to our consultation have suggested that current funding regimes work against the effective embedding of language skills in vocational training and have tended to support discrete, sharply focused provision. There are also some difficult issues in relation to assessment which must be worked through. But it should also be noted that there is a history of effective embedded ESOL in past practice which enabled new arrivals in the UK to access vocational courses while developing their English language skills (for example work by Industrial Language Training (ILT), Shipley College and the Inner London Education Authority (ILEA)). Current funding regimes are not sufficiently flexible to support this type of provision.

We recommend that the DfES and appropriate partners commission a development programme to identify and disseminate effective models and funding approaches for assisting learners with English language learning needs to succeed on vocational programmes.

English for employability

5.9   ESOL provision which includes elements of employability skills is particularly appropriate not only for new arrivals, including adults from the A8 states seeking work, but also for longer-term unemployed refugees and adults from settled communities without a work history or who have been made redundant from declining sectors. For all these learners, language is only one of the needs which must be addressed to enable them to have a good chance of seeking work successfully. There are a number of programmes, for example the Progress GB EQUAL project, which bring together the different elements of the necessary support into holistic programmes which are highly effective in connecting learners to the job market. These programmes depend on effective inter-agency working and include occupational English language, specialised information, advice and guidance (IAG), job-seeking skills, support to secure recognition and conversion of qualifications, training in awareness of the cultures and conventions of UK workplaces, work experience and voluntary work placements.

We recommend that the DfES and appropriate partners should commission work to draw out the lessons from such programmes and that developments on these lines should be explicitly prioritised in funding and planning guidance.

Case study: Integrated employability programme

The Progress GB EQUAL project has brought together partners from six regions and nationally to test and evaluate new ways to improve the employability of refugees and migrant workers. The partners come from the statutory, voluntary, community, FE and private sectors and between them are implementing a range of methods to ensure that refugees and migrants can engage in the workforce at a level commensurate with their skills, experience and qualifications. The approaches, although different in each location, are all holistic and involve a combination of information, advice and guidance, skills auditing, support in the recognition of qualifications and in finding suitable employment.

In some regions/cities a network of information and advice providers has been formed with the ability between the network members to meet all the advice needs of the migrants. Three partners are also developing vocationally specific ESOL in key occupational sectors to help to overcome the language barriers faced by some new arrivals, one of which is described here.

Occupational ESOL is a core element of the NIACE Upskill vocational skills adaptation programme for refugees and migrants with overseas experience in accountancy, business administration, construction and health and social care. It was essential to build occupational ESOL into the programme because occupational language needs can prevent access to appropriate employment and yet are rarely addressed by general ESOL provision. The extent of each participant's occupational language skills needs are identified during an initial wide-ranging skills audit undertaken with a personal adviser. The adviser guides the participant through their process of vocational adaptation over a period of up to 18 months. As well as providing ongoing encouragement, the adviser identifies individually tailored adaptation activities. In addition to occupational ESOL courses, adaptation activities can range across work experience, vocational training, occupational networking and IT training. The project has developed new occupational language courses in administration, accountancy and health and social care. A module within each course covers UK employment application requirements and processes. Highlighting the relevance of the occupational ESOL, gaining endorsements from employers and identifying language needs whilst on work experience has helped to convince participants of the very real need to gain a working knowledge of occupational English.

Progress GB (EQUAL ESF) Development Partnership

5.10 JCP has for the last few years been a major funder of ESOL provision linked to employability as part of its programmes for the unemployed. It will continue to fund ESOL as part of the mandatory New Deal programmes for young people and the long-term unemployed and the voluntary programme for lone parents. But responsibility for much of the provision it previously supported has been transferred to the LSC as a consequence of the 2004 *Welfare to Workforce Development* report which recommended that the LSC should take on lead responsibility for procuring and managing all *Skills for Life* provision. The amount of money being transferred to the LSC with this provision is substantially less than the Department for Work and Pensions allocated to it in their last full year of responsibility. This is a source of grave concern to us. It is all too likely that many of the clients who were the prime target of the JCP provision will not benefit from LSC funding since their learning, usually at Entry Level 3 and below, will not count towards the LSC's PSA targets, quite apart from the inevitable impact of the reduction in funding on the level of provision overall.

5.11 We understand that the LSC and JCP are working together to develop a new programme which will allow JCP customers not on the New Deals greater access, on a voluntary basis, to LSC programmes. The programme is intended to combine employability training with embedded LLN. This is potentially a welcome development for ESOL learners, because adequate language skills are an essential underpinning of sustainable employability.

We recommend that the design of the new LSC employability and ESOL programme should take into account the distinctive needs of ESOL learners, and have both learning and employability outcomes, and ensure that the learning outcomes should address the needs of Entry Level learners as well as higher-level learners who count towards the LSC's current Public Service Agreement (PSA) targets.

5.12 It is essential that in its wider work JCP recognises the importance of language learning for the sustainable employability of its clients with ESOL needs. We have heard of many cases in which people have been forced to abandon language courses before completion in order to take a job, usually at a level below their potential. We understand the pressures on individual JCP advisers to hit job placing targets, but do not think that such actions are in the interests of the long-term employability of the people concerned. JCP should review the instructions to its advisers and ask them always to consider the long-term impact of forcing someone to abandon an ESOL course in order to take up a job.

Workplace ESOL

5.13 Targeted ESOL for workers can be of benefit to migrant workers, refugees and adults from settled communities. Better language skills will improve communications in the work environment, help raise productivity, help raise workers' awareness of their rights and responsibilities at work, and help them get access to the other services they need such as health, housing and education. Organising this provision on work premises is a highly effective approach. However, other solutions are needed to meet the learning needs of workers where this is not practical, for instance where premises are unsuitable or few workers with English language learning needs are employed. There are some excellent examples of good practice supported by employers and, in unionised workplaces, by trades unions. Funding has come from the Union Learning Fund, ESOL Pathfinder funding and the Employer Training Pilots (now replaced by Train to Gain). In this good practice, the curriculum combines language skills with material that relates to both communication at work and wider life needs. This wider focus benefits both the learners, who are able to become more effective members of their communities and more informed service users, and the employer who benefits from a more settled workforce.

Case study: ESOL Workplace – Trades Union Congress

Gunstones Bakeries in Chesterfield is a large food manufacturer employing well over 800 staff, approximately 30 per cent of whom are migrant workers. The union on site, the Bakers, Food and Allied Workers Union, identified huge skills for life needs amongst the workforce and within that a high ESOL need. Union Learning Reps, reflecting the diversity of the workforce, were trained and a learning project took off with full company cooperation. The company was keen to provide for all of its workforce, including new agency staff. Initially provision was enabled through the local Derbyshire Employer Training pilot but when that ended the provision continued with a 50/50 arrangement on paid time for learning negotiated by the union. If it is difficult for individuals to attend in shift time then they are still paid 50 per cent for attendance in their own time. The 130 different shift patterns presented a challenge for timetabling provision. Two-hour workshops were set up to allow for flexible attendance patterns. From October 2005 to July 2006 27 learners, from Pre-Entry level to Level 1, attended. The curriculum was adapted to embed such topics as health and safety and use of metal detection equipment. Accreditation is offered but with complicated attendance and release issues qualification achievement is taking time. Chesterfield College have worked flexibly, changing class times to maximise attendance. The project continues, aiming to enable access to ESOL learning for many more of the workforce.

5.14 Despite these examples of good practice, workplace ESOL remains underdeveloped, and the funding sources noted above are for the most part temporary and ad-hoc. There are a number of significant issues which must be addressed if workplace ESOL is to become a more significant element in provision:

- Employers are not in general aware of the potential benefits to them of making ESOL provision available in the workplace. It is important that there is a sustained publicity effort, drawing on current good practice, to make employers aware of those advantages and to inform them about how they can become involved. It will be particularly important to ensure that SSCs are fully engaged in this area. We have noted that no current Sector Skills Agreements specifically address ESOL, although there are some sectors where it is clearly very relevant. We note that Asset Skills has a lead role in this area, and we would hope to be able to start a dialogue with them to consider how best to ensure appropriate SSC action to support work in this area.

- Small employers will find it particularly difficult to make provision. Learning providers should look for ways of working with groups of small employers to help stimulate the provision of ESOL for their workers.

- There are significant pedagogic issues. Within a single workplace there is likely to be a mix of learning levels and skills, and of learning objectives, which make it difficult to plan and deliver provision. The current qualifications structure will not always be appropriate to the needs of these learners.

- There are also significant practical issues for providers in offering effective workplace-based provision[17] and many are not geared up to meet them. They include the need to fit in with working patterns, and to make provision away from the providers' sites. It is also important to ensure that tutors are properly trained to work in workplace settings.

- It is also important to ensure that there are good progression routes in place for learners who want to move on from workplace-based provision, with appropriate information, advice and guidance.

- It is important to ensure that Union Learning Representatives and brokers understand ESOL issues to inform their negotiations with employees and their employers.

5.15 We have noted above our concern that the transfer of responsibility for all *Skills for Life* provision to the LSC might have an unintended adverse consequence for the important area of ESOL for employability. In addition to the approach we recommend to the new programme which is planned, we believe that is

---

[17] Many of these are identified in the ALI survey report *Skills for Life at Work*.

essential that the LSC gives greater attention to the requirement for work-related ESOL in its planning and policy priorities. To do this effectively it will need to work in close partnership at national, regional and local levels with other government agencies and with major players among commercial and voluntary providers.

We recommend that work-related language training for migrants, refugees and the members of settled communities should be addressed in Regional Economic Strategies and the work of Regional Strategic Partnerships.

5.16 It has been suggested that the Train to Gain scheme provides an appropriate means of addressing some of the needs we have identified, in particular the funding gap in relation to higher-level provision. We do not believe this is so. Our understanding is that the Train to Gain scheme is intended to support adults to their first Level 2 qualification: we believe that higher-level ESOL learners do not fall into this category and their needs should be addressed by a more flexible funding approach. Neither will the designated Train to Gain funding meet the needs of workers who want stand alone ESOL or those with English language learning needs below Level 1, and the constraints on using core funding to providing this have already been identified.

5.17 Improving the quality of workplace-related provision requires some significant underpinning actions to be undertaken:

- As noted above, it is essential to research and publicise the good practice which already exists, to provide guidance on effective organisational models for delivering workplace-related ESOL, from the perspectives of both employers and providers.
- **We recommend that the Quality Improvement Agency (QIA) should commission the development of a curriculum and related materials for workplace-related ESOL** which includes a range of generic workplace culture and communications issues integrated with language learning for different purposes at different levels. The recently developed citizenship materials may be a helpful analogy.
- These issues must also be reflected in the development of teacher training materials, both for new entrants to ESOL teaching and for CPD for experienced teachers. Again we **recommend that the QIA should commission such materials.**

5.18 All these issues have important consequences for the funding of ESOL to which we return in section 9 of our report. We have noted above that we believe that employers who attract migrant workers to the UK should be encouraged to contribute to the costs of appropriate ESOL provision, in relation to the conditions for sponsors of migrant workers and in relation to the Gangmasters registration scheme.

Quality, qualifications and learner support

6

The quality of ESOL provision is variable and not consistently high enough. There should be a thematic inspection of ESOL provision and a continuing programme of research into delivery. The impact of the new ESOL qualifications should be reviewed and they should be promoted to employers, higher education and learners. The relationship of ESOL qualifications to funding targets should be reviewed. We discuss the importance of learner support for ESOL learners and recommend measures to improve it.

6.1 We asked respondents to our questionnaire to set out the key ingredients of excellent teaching and learning. The vision they offered was of ESOL provision which is varied, sparkling, inclusive and relevant, and which challenges learners to achieve and progress. That vision was endorsed by those who commented on our interim report. There is perhaps nothing surprising in this summary, but it is worth keeping in mind as a benchmark as we look at the available evidence on the quality of provision.

6.2 It is important to recognise that ESOL is offered by a wide variety of providers – in FE colleges, local authority adult education, voluntary and community organisations, custodial environments, private training providers – and in a wide variety of settings, some of them far removed from traditional educational settings. So there is a daunting and varied range of challenges to be met if the vision of excellent teaching and learning set out above is to be achieved.

6.3 The message from recent ALI and Ofsted[18] inspections is clear. While there are significant regional variations, across the country too little ESOL provision is good or better, and too much is inadequate. Just under half of ESOL provision in colleges is graded good or better, while in adult and community learning (ACL) it is less than a quarter. In colleges a fifth of ESOL provision is assessed as inadequate and in ACL more than a quarter. These are the settings where most ESOL provision is made: the evidence of low-quality provision is therefore worrying, particularly given the extent of changes in the national framework and the marked growth in ESOL provision which appear not to have brought about any significant general improvement in quality. While there are some encouraging signs of improvement we believe that a strong national evaluation is required to accurately assess the extent of progress, and we recommend this below. It may be that the growth in provision is itself a factor which has made it harder to secure consistent improvements in quality. ESOL is more difficult to deliver than many other curriculum areas: it contains elements of both learning a language and acquiring a basic skill. This makes it particularly difficult to teach, yet there has been little recognition of the specific challenges faced by teachers of ESOL. In addition, ESOL is often managed and inspected alongside other subjects and this has made it difficult to arrive at an overall judgement of the quality of current ESOL teaching. We think it important that the inspectorates give full attention to the difficult quality issues around ESOL and are anxious that the move to reduced intensity inspections should not prevent this. For all these reasons, the Committee believes that this area would benefit from an in-depth review by the inspectorates, and **recommends that ALI and Ofsted should undertake a national survey inspection on the quality of**

---

[18] ALI (Adult Learning Inspectorate) and Ofsted (Office for Standards in Education) are the two inspectorates with responsibility for inspecting the quality of post-16 learning.

ESOL which would analyse existing reports and undertake field visits, with a view to making recommendations, taking into account the recommendations of this Committee. We set out this recommendation in our interim report, and it has been widely welcomed in responses to that document. Implementing this recommendation will require the DfES to commission the inspectorates to carry out such a survey inspection and we hope that they will do so in the next remit letter to the inspectorates.

6.4   We have drawn heavily in this report on the very valuable programme of research undertaken by the NRDC. In looking at the existing evidence on the pedagogy of ESOL and associated issues we were struck by how comparatively under-researched ESOL is, especially in comparison to EFL and literacy. Although we can learn from this research, inevitably questions relating to the field of ESOL, for instance ESOL in the workplace, are not addressed. Yet the complexities of learner needs and profiles, the wide variety of settings in which learning is undertaken and learners' different objectives all mean that more high-quality research would be of immediate relevance and help to practitioners and policy makers alike. The current major NRDC project on ESOL effective practice[19] is therefore of particular importance in relation to quality issues and we have drawn on its emerging findings fully in the recommendations we make in this final report. Its findings raise some important general issues relating to what works to facilitate effective learning. It notes that the longer learners have been in the UK the less likely they are to be making progress, i.e. the earlier provision can be offered the more effective it will be. It also underlines the importance of the expertise and professionalism of teachers and the variety of teaching and learning methods as the major factor in ensuring effective ESOL practice.

We recommend that NRDC should be commissioned to continue and extend its programme of research on ESOL as an essential complement to the thematic inspection of ESOL which we have recommended.

6.5   One important aspect of quality from the learners' perspective is the wide variety of providers. As noted above, this presents challenges to ensuring consistent improvements in quality across the system. But this does not mean that the 'non-standard' providers should be regarded as necessarily sub-standard or dispensable. They are often the only providers able to reach some of the most marginal and disadvantaged learners, often because of their close links to learners' communities, and because they are less intimidating than mainstream educational providers for those prospective learners who do not have extensive or successful educational experience. So if ESOL provision is to meet the needs of all the potential learners it is vital that provision in voluntary and community settings, and in the adult and community education sector is retained and enhanced. Yet these providers are particularly under threat, from the wish of contractors to rely on ever bigger contracts with mainstream providers, from the concentration of funding linked to targets on qualifications beyond the reach of the most vulnerable learners and, in the voluntary and community sector, from the need continually to bid and re-bid for funding simply to stay alive. **We recommend that one of the objectives of the funding arrangements for ESOL should be to ensure a varied network of high-quality providers.** The network must be capable of engaging with the full range of learners and potential learners.

Case study: Provider collaboration

This partnership illustrates a creative solution to reducing the waste of time and valuable resources and frustration for learners and providers caused by learners registering with several providers to maximise their chances of gaining a place. Its broad aims are to improve the uptake of literacy, language and numeracy provision and the achievement and prosperity of local people through learning. Membership is comprised of providers from the FE sector, the local authorities, and the voluntary and community

---

[19]   NRDC ESOL Effective Practice Project (due to complete Summer 2006).

> *sector. Current funding includes annual sponsorship from partner colleges, city council, European Social Fund (ESF) and nextstep information, advice and guidance (IAG) funding. A key activity is BEGIN's support of collaborative work across all sectors to meet the increasing demand for ESOL across the county. Services include a single information point and management of a waiting list and referral system for all English language classes in the conurbation. Essential features are impartial information and advice, a central client database, and central course mapping, appointment and tracking systems. It also functions as a local resource for expertise and information, promotion, planning and capacity building. This includes data sharing and analysis to highlight trends and learner needs for joint planning, workforce development, and other relevant issues.*
>
> BEGIN (Basic Education Guidance in Nottinghamshire) Partnership

6.6 The following paragraphs examine some of the key features of good and bad practice: retention, qualifications, assessment, support for learners, use of information technology, and learning difficulties or disabilities.

Retention

6.7 In our interim report we noted the importance of retention and encouraging learner persistence on their learning journey. This is a particular concern for ESOL provision, perhaps unsurprisingly given that learners usually have a range of circumstances in their lives, including geographical mobility (sometimes enforced by dispersal policy), which impact on their ability to establish regular patterns of attendance. This adds weight to the view that a prime requirement of ESOL provision is that there should be a wide variety of types of provision in terms of setting and learning style to cater for the variation in learners' circumstances: appropriate provision, including effective support services such as childcare and help with transport, will encourage them to complete their courses. For those learners in work, effective and continuing links with their employers are essential. We have more to say below about support for learners. Provision must be flexible enough to respond to the needs of learners whose situations may not allow them to attend classes regularly for sustained periods of time.

Qualifications

6.8 Where learners are entered for externally accredited qualifications, pass rates are usually high. New ESOL qualifications have only recently been introduced and it is too soon to make a definitive assessment of their effectiveness. These qualifications are based on the ESOL core curriculum and aligned with the levels defined in the national standards for adult literacy and numeracy; Entry Levels 1, 2 and 3, and Levels 1 and 2. ESOL *Skills for Life* certificates are now available in Speaking and Listening, Reading, and Writing.

6.9 Many respondents to our questionnaire viewed the new framework as helpful, particularly welcoming the fact that, in contrast to the National Test in Literacy which tests only certain reading skills, the new structure offers certification in the four skills of speaking, listening, reading and writing. Most learners find accreditation motivating and welcome the opportunity to set themselves against a national standard, and common standards are useful in helping devise clear progression routes and to map progress. The modular format helps in enabling learners with 'spiky' profiles to get proper recognition for their achievements.

6.10 But a number of comments on our interim report set out some important concerns. Some of these stem from the very complex history of the development of the qualifications and the number of players (the DfES *Skills for Life* Strategy Unit, QCA and the LSC) involved: a number of respondents to our interim report felt that there had been insufficient communication between those players and with expert practitioners to ensure that the development process was transparent and the result fully understood by the sector. We think it essential to the acceptance of the new qualifications and any future developments that there are effective communications with the sector. We also note that the resulting qualifications arrangements are confusing for both learners and providers and believe that it is important that they are simplified and effectively promoted. This has to be a joint effort between the main players. In paragraph 3.21 we recommend the setting up of a joint forum on ESOL involving the key players involved. We believe that the subject of qualifications should be an early topic for such a body. Such a discussion would, of course, need to involve the awarding bodies and representatives of practitioners.

6.11   There are also emerging concerns about the impact of the new qualifications in practice. Some awarding bodies felt that in the negotiations over the new qualifications, the QCA had been insufficiently sensitive to the specific requirements of the full range of ESOL learners.

6.12   Learners gain a full qualification when they have achieved units in each of the modes, with a notional hundred hours of learning attached to each level. Some practitioners feel that the steps in the qualifications structure are too large and therefore inappropriate for many learners, who are unlikely to be able to undertake the assumed 300 hours of learning if they are only able to study part time, or if they are unable to read or write in any language, as is the case for many ESOL learners. A greater degree of unitisation to recognise smaller steps in learning would be helpful. These smaller steps would assist and motivate learners by recognising smaller chunks of learning, especially those wanting to transfer credit when they move from one place to another. Mutual recognition between awarding bodies would be very helpful in this context. Mobility, sometimes enforced, is a key characteristic of some ESOL learners. Many would welcome the development of accreditation arrangements to recognise the achievements of learners who are working towards Entry Level 1. At the other end of the scale there is a lack of appropriate ESOL qualifications at Levels 3 and 4, in particular for progression to higher education (HE). The full range of IELTS, for instance, is not recognised within *Skills for Life* because of the Level 2 ceiling, but is required by many learners, whether for employment where, for instance, it is an entry requirement to medical professions, or for entry to HE. We believe that if ESOL provision is to have the optimum impact on economic performance and on individuals' life chances, some means of funding qualifications at these higher levels must be available. We return to this question in section 9.

6.13   There is little evidence that the *Skills for Life* qualifications have yet gained any currency with employers or HE bodies and they are not recognised internationally. In part this is no doubt a consequence of their novelty and the lack of evidence of their effectiveness. **We recommend that the impact of the new ESOL learner qualifications should be assessed** – the take-up, the destination of learners in terms both of work and further education and training, and the effect on providers, teachers and the organisation of provision. This work will be important to ensure that the new suite of qualifications meets the full range of learner need. When that information is available, **we recommend that the DfES and QCA should consider how best to promote the new qualifications to learners, employers, higher education and the professions.**

6.14   One of the consequences of the lack of currency of the new qualifications is that in the global context of increasingly mobile populations, some learners prefer the international examinations to the *Skills for Life* ESOL qualifications. This includes learners who qualify as *Skills for Life* learners but find the *Skills for Life* qualifications do not meet their needs for work or progression purposes or who are likely to spend some time working or studying internationally even where their permanent base is Britain. Inevitably there will be overlap in the backgrounds, motivations and circumstances of people who make different choices.

6.15   The unintended impact of the qualifications system on the funding for ESOL and the consequences for quality also causes concern. Whilst practitioners welcome the greater relevance for learners of accrediting all four skills, there is a funding anomaly between ESOL and literacy. The only accredited provision that counts towards the *Skills for Life* national targets is a full award at Entry Level 3, Level 1 and Level 2 in either literacy or ESOL. If learners achieve a literacy qualification, this full award is the national test in literacy, but if they achieve an ESOL qualification a full award means achievement in all four skills. The national test in literacy element is common to both awards. From a learner's point of view the ESOL award is more rounded and appropriate, but from a provider's position ESOL accreditation costs more to achieve the same funding. There is some evidence that providers are, as a consequence, using the literacy qualification inappropriately for ESOL learners. **We recommend that the disparity between the assessment requirements of literacy and ESOL qualifications in relation to the national *Skills for Life* targets should be corrected.**

6.16 Some concern was expressed that entering learners for separate accreditation for speaking and listening, reading and writing imposed a heavy burden, both financial and administrative, on providers. Other concerns were expected about the process of dealing with entries, the conduct of awards, and ensuring that enrolments and accreditation matched in course documentation and LSC returns. Some suggested that learners should be required to contribute to these costs, but we are not persuaded that this would be universally appropriate. More significant is the cost to the public purse, and the issue of which learners should be required to contribute to the overall cost of their tuition: we return to this below.

Planning and assessment

6.17 Respondents to our questionnaire universally recognised that initial, formative and summative assessment are all central to effective provision. The effectiveness of such assessment is rightly one of the key concerns of Ofsted and ALI inspectors. A major element of the *Skills for Life* infrastructure is the Individual Learning Plan (ILP), a document owned by the learner to be used as a tool for identifying learning needs, planning learning to meet these needs and recording progress and achievement. It usually takes the form of a number of negotiated individual learning outcomes. Although providers are expected to carry out initial, formative and summative assessment, there is no requirement to use any particular recording format. However, evidence submitted to the inquiry suggests widespread expectations from inspectors and requirements from ESOL managers to produce ILPs based on inappropriate models. This caused concerns which were clearly strongly felt by many teachers.

6.18 A number of respondents to the questionnaire, and the participants in some of our focus groups, expressed concerns about the appropriateness of this approach for ESOL learners, and about the tendency of both managers and inspectors to regard this as the only acceptable evidence of good practice on assessment. Some of the pressure to produce ILPs was a consequence of the funding regime which was in place before the introduction of the new ESOL qualifications: this pressure should no longer apply. But the wider concern about ILPs was reiterated in our literature review and in responses to our interim report in which we set out the debate. The main anxiety was the complexity of the forms which have been produced and the burden placed on both learners and teachers in their completion. It is recognised that there is no single standardised approach to ILPs for ESOL learners. But the concern is that the approach is inappropriate to the learning pattern of most ESOL learners as it does not take account of group learning outcomes, is often too detailed on specific language items, and does not support the need continuously to reinforce language structures and their use in different societal and cultural contexts.

6.19 Effectively managing ILPs in the large groups typical in ESOL poses a particular challenge because of the huge amounts of bureaucracy they entail. Some practitioners argue that the ILP process is not helpful to lower-level ESOL learners because they do not have the language skills to be able to negotiate appropriate ILPs and they struggle to understand the ILP which is produced. But these negative views were not universal: some respondents saw ILPs as a useful support to ensuring individuals' needs were met within group learning situations and thought they had had a positive impact on standards. They were seen as particularly useful for learners at Level 2 and full-time adult learners, although their impact on part-time adult learners was thought to be limited. All respondents recognised the importance of identifying learning aims and recognising progress and achievement, and suggested alternatives such as adopting RARPA[20] processes or a process based on regular individual and/or group tutorials.

6.20 Recent research, including forthcoming NRDC publications, provides further helpful evidence on the use of ILPs. This echoes the anxiety expressed in responses to our questionnaire that the ILP focus on individual language learning goals and SMART targets (Specific, Measurable, Achievable, Realistic, Time-related) were inappropriate in the ESOL context which relies heavily on group processes and classroom interaction. Indeed, some argue that the use of SMART targets is at odds with the way in which learners actually acquire language skills because they result in a model of language acquisition as a linear process in which identifiable skills can be broken down into small separate items that can be expressed as measurable, time-bound targets and learned in sequence. In contrast, theorists of second language acquisition contend that successful language learning relies on constant and consistent revisiting language in contexts and alongside other skills. This is not easy to measure as separate units of learning, so does not align with ILP processes commonly used.

6.21 The problems are more acute at Entry Levels 1 and 2 when learners do not have sufficient language skills to be able to articulate and negotiate their language learning goals. There were also serious concerns about the burden on learners and teachers of agreeing the required range of targets within ILPs. The research found that tutorial processes were most effective for planning learning and recognising progress. There is no standard ILP format, and it is clear that much effort has been expended on developing home-made forms: there was a clear demand for further guidance on good practice in ESOL ILPs. We note the work that the NRDC, alongside ALI and Ofsted, are undertaking on the ILP process. We believe that it is important to build on this and look at the ILP process in the specific context of ESOL. **We recommend that the appropriateness for ESOL learners, particularly at lower levels, of the ILP process should be reviewed.** Such a review should take account of the need to ensure that learning is properly planned and that the mechanisms, including tutorials, used are practicable and appropriate to the skills and needs of learners and to ESOL pedagogy. This review should result in the issue of practical guidance to ESOL teachers in all sectors and clear statements of good practice. Such a review could usefully build on the NRDC research.

Curriculum and materials

6.22 The ESOL core curriculum document sets out in detail the competences that adults should be taught to enable them to reach the national literacy standards, with examples of the contexts in which they could be developed. It is designed to support teachers to design learning programmes and assess learners' starting points, development aims, progress and achievement. It has been broadly welcomed as it provides a framework with standardised skills descriptors for different levels. It provides an invaluable resource to assist new entrants to the profession and a reference point for experienced teachers.

6.23 However, some limitations of particular relevance to the ESOL environment (although not exclusive to it) have been noted. The cultural and social dimensions of language use and their place in language learning are not explored in any depth, although some contexts are suggested and the document stresses that teachers should use situations and activities to meet the interests of the learners they are working with. This means that the curriculum can lead to programmes more related to skills than to real-life social interaction. Inspectors have registered concerns that some teachers are using it too rigidly rather than

---

[20] RARPA is a framework for recognising progress and achievement in non-accredited learning: 'Recognising and recording progress and achievement'.

adapting and using it creatively to satisfy learners' needs, and researchers have similarly suggested that some inexperienced teachers rely too heavily on the core curriculum (ALI, 2005; Baynham *et al.*, forthcoming). This is arguably an inevitable consequence where new teachers lack training to develop imaginative and flexible approaches to designing learning content based on an understanding of the cultural and societal elements of language.

6.24   A further consideration is whether so called 'soft' skills should be an integral part of an ESOL curriculum. Learning to learn, building confidence and self-esteem, developing critical awareness and skills for critical reflection are important skills that underpin both the learning process and the use of new skills and knowledge autonomously in real-life situations (DfES, 2003a; Dutton *et al.*, 2005): some, though not all, ESOL learners will need help in acquiring them. These skills are linked to language skills development and valued by learners. Little attention has been paid to defining these skills, establishing how they can be developed through the learning process and, conversely, whether and how they support language skills development and the ways in which they enable learners to put their skills development into practice in real situations. This could provide a fruitful topic for future research.

6.25   ESOL materials have been developed through a number of initiatives including the *Skills for Life* and Citizenship projects, and many teachers use published EFL materials. These have strengths and limitations. They are often high quality materials but cover a limited range of themes and situations, and lack of work-related materials covering the range of generic and occupation-specific knowledge and communication situations is a particular gap. EFL materials are often not relevant, or are used in ways that fail to stretch, interest and inspire learners (Roberts *et al.*, 2004).

Learner support

6.26   The complex and difficult personal circumstances and varied backgrounds of many ESOL learners mean that effective learner support is a particularly critical issue. A range of distinct roles can be identified:

- Effective support in the form of IAG is essential both before the programme begins, as learners progress and to identify progression routes.
- During the programme individuals will often need support in the form of pastoral support with both personal and learning problems, to help them deal with difficult personal circumstances, in terms of key practical difficulties such as housing and health, and in terms of their own legal status. This work inevitably involves close working with a range of statutory and voluntary agencies.
- There is a role for classroom assistants in discrete ESOL provision and for teachers trained in ESOL in providing additional language support in vocational or embedded provision.
- Learners are also likely to need wider support, in the form of help to get employment, liaison with agencies such as JCP and voluntary agencies working with such groups as refugees, liaison with employers and with community groups.
- Support workers (known by such titles as outreach workers, learning champions and ambassadors) are often also involved in outreach work with groups in the community, attracting new learners and supporting former learners to progress to the next stages of learning.
- Union Learning Representatives and learning brokers perform a similar role in workplaces. They also negotiate provision with employers and providers.

6.27   This is a complex range of requirements, and the needs are often not just complex but also acute. The demands made on providers for support are correspondingly heavy. There is no single optimum way of providing the support that ESOL learners need: the circumstances and the resources available in particular cases will determine the best approach. There are some excellent examples of good practice and these should be more widely known.

Case study: ESOL specialist learner support

One approach to providing the full range of support to ESOL learners adopted by a Local Authority adult learning service is to appoint a dedicated Learner Support Organiser (LSO). The post holder is a qualified, experienced ESOL teacher with specialist IAG skills who has an in-depth understanding of the needs of ESOL learners. Specialist IAG makes the vital link between settlement needs and language learning, benefiting both the learner and the ESOL provider through strengthening recruitment, retention, achievement and progression.

The support is closely linked to learning through a learner support section on ILPs which links agreed action plans with classroom language learning. An external speaker programme and local materials support learner progression and settlement, and the Learner Resource Centre contains materials on local services, educational and careers information, and job vacancies. A major objective of the LSO post is liaison with external agencies to secure a smooth transition into appropriate learning, training and employment opportunities for ESOL learners. Learner feedback, progression reports, case studies and ALI inspection reports are used to monitor and evaluate the work. Outcomes include maintenance of regular attendance leading to accreditation, progression to other courses and vocational training, voluntary and paid employment. Wider benefits include community engagement, integration of new arrivals, and promotion of ESOL provision through case studies and role models.

Leicester Adult Education College

6.28 Inevitably many of these demands fall on the teachers themselves. This can be a particular challenge for teachers from the same communities as the learners, who face high level of demand inside and outside their work. There are concerns that staff often lack expertise in areas which are important to ESOL learners, such as rights, entitlements, regulations relating to immigration status, the right to work and access to funding and learning opportunities. It is not realistic to expect colleges or teachers of ESOL to be equipped to tackle the full range of learners' needs, but it is realistic to expect them to be aware of how those needs can be addressed and to have in place arrangements to ensure effective links with other sources of advice and support. At the least it is essential that all frontline staff need language and cultural awareness training in order that hesitant learners do not fall at the first hurdle.

6.29 Effective IAG is important for all learners, not least ESOL learners. **We recommend that the current DfES review of IAG services should urgently look at the needs of ESOL learners.** Such a review should consider the needs of ESOL learners for IAG related to employability and their wider needs as well as learning needs. Many ESOL learners need IAG in their first languages and the review should consider how this can most effectively be made available. Even where colleges have specialist support services, learners are sometimes reluctant to use them and prefer to go to the teachers they know and trust. It is important that providers carefully review their capacity to provide the IAG services required by ESOL learners, looking not only at the resources available in-house and how well they are deployed, but also ensuring that there are effective links to external specialist agencies and support services for those learners who need them. It is important that specialist IAG and other support, such as counselling, is given by workers with training, experience and skills specific to the needs of ESOL learners. It will also be important to ensure that JCP advisers are aware of the needs of ESOL learners and how to ensure that they are effectively addressed. It is for consideration whether the Matrix standard should be revised to include evidence of capacity to address ESOL issues among the points considered in assessing IAG providers against the standard. **We recommend that the Matrix standard should require that candidates who advise ESOL learners are properly briefed and trained to enable them to respond knowledgeably and effectively to their specific circumstances and requirements. We also recommend that the survey inspection proposed by the Committee should examine in particular how appropriately skilled and qualified learning assistants, learning support workers and teaching**

assistants can be used effectively to support programmes. When the inspection is complete, QIA should identify models of effective practice and ensure their dissemination. This work can helpfully build on the work which LLUK have been commissioned by DfES to undertake on the range of support roles across the *Skills for Life* programme. This work is welcome, but we believe that it is essential that it should include an ESOL-specific element.

ESOL for learners with difficulties or disabilities

6.30 A number of adults seeking English language provision have physical disabilities, mental ill health or learning difficulties, especially amongst refugee and asylum seeker populations because of the experiences, traumas and torture they have undergone. This has profound implications for them as learners and for the institutions providing learning. They need support and guidance to identify appropriate strategies to respond, but there is a serious shortage of research, and as yet few robust and consistent mechanisms for sharing practice. The recent publication of guidance on good practice in English language provision for learners with learning difficulties or disabilities developed through the DfES Pathfinder project should do a great deal to support developments (DfES, 2006a).

6.31 The area of disability and ethnicity is complex: there are many problematic issues and questions but few definitive answers. Cultural beliefs and perceptions can influence how disability is defined, attitudes to disability, and how people define themselves and, therefore, the extent to which learners either acknowledge or disclose their disability and the extent to which they are willing to seek assistance. These factors can be complicated where language skills affect communication. All teachers, advisers and support workers need awareness of these factors as well as strategies for navigating this difficult terrain. The question of whether ESOL or other specialist programmes is the most appropriate provision can be complicated, and referral might depend on the first point of contact. ESOL, disability and dyslexia specialists do not always have training in assessment skills to enable them to identify needs in the other areas, and their difficulties are compounded when working with beginner ESOL learners, who have very limited oral skills. As a result referral might not meet needs or learners might not receive appropriate support and leave the class because of frustrations with progress. **We recommend that there should be training for ESOL teachers on the new guidance on disability and how effectively to share assessment strategies in relation to ESOL learners with learning difficulties or disabilities across their organisations.**

6.32 We welcome the fact that DfES has commissioned LLUK to develop a qualifications pathway for *Skills for Life* work with learners with learning difficulties or disabilities. We believe that this work should include an ESOL-specific component.

Information technology

6.33 There is no doubt about the enormous potential of ICT to enhance language learning, demonstrated in the ESOL context by the Pathfinder projects in which the use of ICT was popular with learners and had the potential to improve achievement rates when used well. Learners need both to learn to use ICT and to use ICT to learn. In an under-skilled workforce in which there may be many ESOL learners, ICT in itself is a crucial skill. But for learners linguistic competence will be critical to their success in using ICT for learning. They must be familiar with the language associated with technology as well as having sufficient language skills to access and navigate computer functions and programmes. Knowledge of ICT skills is also important to enable them to take full advantage of technology to enhance and support progress in their English language learning.

6.34   There is a great deal of active development work going on in the area of ICT and learning (for example, in development of ESOL e-learning materials for use by ACL providers[21] and an EQUAL action research project into e- and mobile ESOL learning for job searches in the health and social care sector) and much excellent practice. But there are some important practical issues to be considered. It is clear that the availability of both hardware and software is patchy, particularly in non-mainstream settings. Even where there is availability, teachers need to acquire the necessary skills to use ICT in the learning situation. For teachers, staff development is critical to acquiring the skills essential to effective implementation of ICT. It is welcome that ICT is being included in the DfES review of the minimum core for all *Skills for Life* teachers. There is a need to build on existing research into the most effective pedagogic approaches to the use of ICT for ESOL, and there is likely to be much to be learned from the use of ICT in other curricular areas. We note that NRDC have recently completed a study on effective practice in ICT: a majority of the sites in which the development work took place were ESOL providers. We welcome the fact that this study (and the other effective practice studies which NRDC has undertaken) is to be followed up by the production of a practitioner guide.

---

[21]   See the NIACE website for details of ICT learning work: http://www.niace.org.uk/Research/ICT/projects.htm

7

Teacher supply, initial training and continuing professional development

Recruiting, training and retaining sufficient qualified teachers to deal with the expansion in provision described in previous sections poses significant challenges. The supply of initial teacher training places has not kept pace with the huge demand created by the expansion of provision over the last five years, there are worries about the quality of some teacher training provision, and there is a continuing need for relevant continuing professional development (CPD) for experienced ESOL teachers. Strategies to meet these challenges are being developed in the context of broader reforms in post-16 teacher education. These form a fast-changing context to the matters discussed in this section: initial teacher training, CPD and teacher supply.

ESOL teaching qualifications

7.1 The *Skills for Life* strategy specified that all new literacy, numeracy and ESOL tutors should work towards a specialist teaching qualification. New specialist qualifications were developed to sit alongside the generic Certificate for Teachers in Further Education. The ESOL subject specifications set out the linguistic knowledge and understanding and personal language skills required at Levels 3 and 4 (DfES/FENTO, 2002), and since September 2003 all new entrants to ESOL teaching have been expected to acquire them. There is currently some confusion about the application of the Level 3 specifications, and we hope this will be clarified by the current review of the needs of vocational teachers and the support worker role being conducted by LLUK.[22] We understand that LLUK are developing standards and qualifications frameworks for teachers and learning support separately. They will develop appropriate CPD qualifications at appropriate level(s) for these staff within the relevant framework. This approach is consistent with our view that an increase in embedded ESOL and more effective language support for learners in vocational classes are important priorities. Research indicates that language support and embedded provision must be led by a teacher with specialist qualifications. However, the subject tutors must also have understanding and awareness of the ways in which they can make an effective contribution.

7.2 *Success for All*, published in 2002, recommended that by 2010 all teachers working in the learning and skills sector should be trained and qualified (DfES, 2002). Subsequently, a framework for the reform of initial teacher training for all new entrants to the profession and for ongoing professional development has been developed (DfES, 2004). ESOL teacher training will be incorporated in this structure which is based on a model of initial teacher training underpinned by the new generic professional standards for teachers in the learning and skills sector currently being devised, followed by ongoing professional development throughout a teacher's career.

---

22 LLUK is the Sector Skills Council for Lifelong Learning.

7.3 The view of the NRDC ESOL Effective Practice research project that the most important factor in effective provision is the expertise and professionalism of teachers is widely echoed in the responses to our questionnaire. It is clear from those responses that a significant number of areas have a shortage of qualified teachers (although in a few areas there are more teachers than jobs). There is widespread agreement that provision should only be delivered by specialist qualified English language teachers who have training and/or experience in linking language development to the different contexts of ESOL learners' lives and that appropriate expectations of minimum entry standards are in place. In practice, inexperienced teachers are often recruited to meet growing demand and this has an adverse impact on quality. Evidence submitted to the inquiry indicated that in some areas there is an insufficient supply of teacher education courses. The DfES *Skills for Life* Strategy Unit acknowledges that data on the nature of the workforce has not been robust enough to inform the planning of supply to meet demand, on a national and regional basis. It is committed to achieving a fully qualified teaching workforce by 2010 and has commissioned LLUK to research workforce characteristics to support planning.

7.4 There is considerable concern about the requirement that *all* specialist ESOL teachers need to gain the newly introduced qualifications: this is seen both as unnecessary for the teachers themselves who are already qualified, with qualifications predating the introduction of the standardised National Qualifications Framework (NQF) (known as 'legacy' qualifications), and as absorbing resources which could otherwise be used to train new recruits. Current arrangements for accreditation of prior experience and learning (APEL) do not seem to be sufficiently attractive to existing teachers to help address this problem.

7.5 Since September 2003 new ESOL teachers entering the profession have been required to hold or obtain two qualifications:

- A stage 3 teaching qualification based on the FENTO *Standards for Teaching and Learning* at Level 4 of the NQF
- A qualification at Level 4 based on the FENTO *Subject Specifications for Teacher of ESOL*

These two qualifications are offered as one integrated programme by some universities and awarding bodies.

7.6 Although there are no formal requirements for existing teachers to re-qualify to gain these new qualifications, DfES states that:

> *It is expected that over time, in the interests of parity and equal opportunity, and in the light of the requirements of the statutory inspection regime as set out in the Common Inspection Framework, existing adult literacy and numeracy and ESOL teachers will take up opportunities to obtain the new specialist qualifications as part of their continuing professional development.* (2003b)

7.7 In our interim report we noted that there is some evidence that providers, in particular FE colleges, concerned with meeting their *Success for All* targets, were putting pressure on teachers with legacy qualifications to take the new qualifications. This can result in the anomalous position that experienced teachers with NQF Level 7 diploma qualifications are having to attend NQF Level 4/5 Certificate in Education courses, apparently for the sole purpose of enabling their employer to meet targets. Since we published our interim report LLUK has published the details of its Professional Recognition Learning and Skills Scheme (PRLS). In our interim report we recommended that consideration should be given to allowing holders of TESOL diplomas to be considered as qualified for the purpose of the *Success for All* targets. We therefore welcome the introduction of the PRLS, and note indications that the adjudication process will acknowledge that ordinarily diploma holders will easily demonstrate subject knowledge. However, we note that the scheme runs only until September 2007 and remain concerned that any successor arrangements should not re-impose unnecessary burdens on holders of TESOL qualifications. It is also important that alongside these arrangements experienced teachers have the opportunity to assess their needs for continuing professional development and support in addressing them.

7.8 APEL offers a different pathway, although PRLS could offer a more accessible route for the majority of teachers until 2007. The introduction of the new teacher qualifications framework from September 2007 should allow the more widespread use of APEL and, furthermore, the development of individualised pathways appropriate to sector, subject and need.

Evidence to our committee suggests that past experience in this area has been disappointing. Good APEL systems are rightly rigorous in their approach, but the effect of the current arrangements has been that many candidates have taken the view that they are more time consuming than taking a course, even though the course is likely to be of little real benefit to them. It is important that APEL systems, while remaining rigorous, should be sufficiently user-friendly to enable teachers with relevant qualifications and experience to gain appropriate recognition for them. The development of top-up modules for diploma holders by two of the awarding bodies is a positive approach. These offer relevant opportunities to update knowledge, skills and gain a recognised *Skills for Life* teaching qualification. Consideration should also be given to the wider recognition of overseas qualifications as another approach to securing more qualified teachers.

7.9 There are currently two routes to qualification; integrated or separate. Training which integrates the generic and subject specialist requirements is generally agreed to be the more effective model, and is the one most commonly adopted in well-established ESOL teacher education.[23] Subject-specific teacher training is also the preferred delivery option of LLUK in its proposals for September 2007, and it is working with the QIA to support providers to ensure as many courses are available in September 2007 as possible.

7.10 There will always be teachers who wish to make a career change into ESOL, whether from EFL or from an unrelated subject area. In the latter case they may have done a Cert. Ed./PGCE in another subject and will need to take a subject specialist course to include ESOL pedagogy. In the former case they may have a good knowledge of English language teaching pedagogy but have little cultural awareness of ESOL client groups and the pedagogical implications of working with different groups of learners. Concerns remain about how teachers transferring to ESOL will acquire the specialist ESOL knowledge and teaching skills they need, and it is important that the new teaching qualifications are flexible enough to allow for both of these groups of teachers to re-qualify in ESOL.

7.11 The rapid expansion of ESOL has meant that large numbers of inexperienced and less-well-qualified staff have been taken on to help providers meet growing demand. In 2003 Ofsted recommended that all *Skills for Life* teachers should have initial training before taking responsibility for teaching learners (Ofsted, 2003). This is not the norm in FE where staff with vocational expertise and experience are employed, then undertake their initial teacher training while in service. They often have experience of training colleagues or trainees. Most prospective ESOL teachers do not arrive with this type of professional identity, and fluency in English alone does not help anyone to know how to start teaching the language. Colleges with established ESOL departments recognise this and usually require an ESOL teaching certificate as a minimum qualification for employment. We agree that pre-service training is essential for ESOL teachers and note that the DfES has commissioned LLUK to pilot a model for pre-entry part-time provision.

We recommend that as pre-service training routes to employment are introduced, employers should be actively discouraged from employing new ESOL teachers who are unqualified.

---

[23] Forthcoming NRDC research found no examples of separated ESOL teacher education programmes at the time of drawing the research sample in 2003.

7.12 It is particularly important that teachers have access to high-quality IAG, given the complexity and fluidity of the current position on qualifications and the new and changing challenges which they face. We support the developments through LLUK and QIA to build capacity for *Skills for Life* IAG and *Skills for Life* teachers.

7.13 The new Professional Standards for Teachers, Tutors and Trainers are to be published in September 2006, and the strategy of Standards Verification UK, the endorsing body, is that the last date for starting courses which meet the existing standards should be September 2006 for two-year programmes and April 2007 for programmes of one year or less. This gives higher education institutions (HEIs) and awarding bodies less than two years to develop new courses, have them validated and accredited and obtain approval for them, a process that normally takes at least two years. There is considerable concern in the field and among awarding bodies and HEIs that there is a real danger that no courses meeting the new standards will be in place before September 2007. We have been assured by DfES that new specialist training provision will be in place for September 2007. We welcome this assurance but remain concerned that this timetable is very demanding. Not only must the new qualifications be in place: so must the necessary support mechanisms in awarding bodies and providers. It would be very damaging to the long-term success of the new qualifications, for which there is widespread support, if they were introduced in a rush and thereby discredited. **We recommend that progress towards introduction of the new qualifications is kept under close scrutiny and that, if there is any danger that they cannot be fully and effectively implemented to the current timetable, urgent consideration should be given to extending the cut-off date for teacher training courses meeting the current standards, to avoid a lacuna of courses in September 2007.**

Continuing professional development (CPD)

7.14 All teachers must have initial teacher training. It is equally important to address the ongoing professional development needs of experienced and new ESOL teachers to ensure that they keep their knowledge and skills up to date and bring informed and creative approaches to teaching English language. CPD has been offered to ensure that teachers are aware of *Skills for Life* requirements. Other CPD is needed to inspire high quality pedagogic practice, and equip teachers moving to work in new types of settings or with different learners. Although CPD is currently available, the offer is not systematic and differs between areas so that not all teachers have access to the training they require. We understand that ESOL CPD has been identified as important by the QIA.

7.15 Additional layers of context-specific knowledge are also needed to supplement pedagogic expertise. It is important to equip staff to recognise and understand the purposes, priorities and language learning needs of individuals from a range of backgrounds learning in a diverse settings including workplaces, communities or prisons. Arguably, most initial training uses FE as a default model so that teachers need additional preparation for teaching in other settings which are often more challenging environments in which to work (Mallows, 2006). They need knowledge to equip them to negotiate the organisational cultures found in locations such as schools, workplaces or prisons, and awareness of how learning in regeneration areas fits with the sustainable communities principals often adopted by other organisations in these settings.

7.16 These needs can be met by increasing the availability of CPD: it is clear that this is attractive to teachers. For example, LLU+'s ESOL network attracts upwards of sixty teachers to its termly meetings. The annual conference of NATECLA (National Association for Teachers of English and other Community Languages to Adults) attracts around 200 participants, many of them self-funded, each year. There is clearly an appetite for CPD which is focused on ESOL teachers' needs and is relevant and credible. But there are some important concerns to be addressed. It is clearly essential to consider how the provision of CPD can be managed in the contexts of existing workloads. There are particular questions concerning how CPD can be offered to part-time workers, many of whom will work for more than one employer, and often for organisations in the voluntary and community sector without the infrastructure themselves to provide or pay for appropriate CPD. One approach might be to put together local networks for the provision of CPD, involving all the local ESOL providers, and we welcome the fact that the DfES has included regional support and networks for both CPD and professional IAG as part of the *Skills for life* Quality Improvement Programme. **We recommend that consideration should be given to offering small amounts of core funding support to appropriate voluntary professional support organisations and peer group networks to enable them to maintain and expand their provision of CPD. Ways should also be developed of helping colleagues and other providers to share expertise.**

Capacity

7.17 Ofsted has identified 'a serious shortage of specialist teachers … in this rapidly expanding sector'. The problem is particularly acute in London, where the London Strategic Unit estimates that some 500 new ESOL teachers will be required every year to meet demand. There are also shortages of teachers in regions where there has not hitherto been large demand for ESOL, for instance in rural areas large numbers of migrant worker are now filling agricultural jobs. A key difficulty is that the available information on the supply of teachers and their qualifications is very patchy which makes planning nationally and within regions very difficult. In our interim report we recommended a snapshot survey of the ESOL workforce to provide a proper benchmark for the development of workforce policy. We therefore welcome the DfES's intention to undertake a survey to estimate the number of unqualified *Skills for Life* teachers in 2006 and 2009. The first snapshot, which will include the characteristics of the ESOL workforce, will report in January 2007. LLUK's continuing programme of data collection will include data on the ESOL workforce which will provide a continuing basis on which the position can be monitored. The issue of workforce data is a concern for the whole of the post-compulsory sector: while we welcome the DFES's and LLUK's current intentions, it is very important that there is a regular supply of reliable data on workforce information, and that the data is used in effective planning at national and regional levels.

7.18 The arguments in the recent FE White Paper (DfES, 2006b) about the importance of professional development apply also to ESOL. One of the reasons for the current shortage is the huge turnover in ESOL teachers.[24] It is difficult to avoid the conclusion that the lack of a clear career structure and the temporary and part-time character of many ESOL jobs are likely to be contributory factors, and that if these concerns are not addressed it will be difficult to reverse the current position. One teacher told us he was looking for employment outside teaching because

> '..there is no long term future. I am cheap labour and end up doing more work than the contract implies. There is little incentive to remain within the sector or teaching.'[25]

7.19 We recognise, of course, that there are many ESOL teachers who do not want, or could not undertake, full-time jobs, but others employed on part-time sessional contracts accept this work because it is all that is offered rather than as a deliberate choice. Respondents to our survey valued the freedom to pursue other interests, but for most this advantage was outweighed by the disadvantages of lack of security, financial instability, and worse employment conditions and less access to training than full-time teachers. Part-time sessional employment is no reason why staff skills and experience should be undervalued and lost to management roles, nor why they should find it difficult to access the necessary professional

---

24 As an illustration, when NIACE approached teachers on the waiting list for curriculum training, they found that approximately 30 per cent had moved jobs.

25 Quote from an informal survey carried out by the Committee that asked ESOL teachers about the advantages and disadvantages of their job.

development. Particular attention should be given to the needs of part-timers (not just in ESOL) in the work currently in hand on remodelling the post-compulsory education workforce. It is also important that where possible, more permanent positions are created to encourage teachers to enter the ESOL specialism. Developing and sustaining a stable workforce is likely to help raise quality as teachers would participate in more professional development. It would also reduce the pressure on training places created by the need to train large numbers of part-time staff discussed below. **We recommend that incentives should be introduced to encourage employers to introduce a more secure career structure for ESOL teachers and increase the proportion of teachers employed on permanent contracts.** A lead agency should be identified to work with relevant bodies and employers. It may be appropriate for the government to set a target in this area to which the responsible bodies and employers are required to work.

7.20   The current shortage is compounded by a shortage of teacher training places and of pre-service training provision. This is not universal across the country: indeed in some areas courses have been postponed or cancelled due to lack of take-up. Again information on what is available is patchy: there is a case for this question to be included in the context of the survey referred to above. But this problem will only be effectively addressed if there are regional strategies for both the recruitment and training of ESOL teachers, involving the major ESOL providers, the providers of teacher training, both initial and CPD, and the key funding bodies. This should be a linked with the regional planning which we have recommended for ESOL provision in para 3.12 of this report.

> *'I'd like to add a comment about ESOL teaching. I'm brand new to the concept, having spent a couple of weeks informally helping a Polish migrant worker improve his English and navigate around our somewhat baffling bureaucratic system. I enjoyed it all so much that I want to train as an ESOL teacher – but can I find a local course? I cannot. Can I find a useful local website? I cannot. I've gathered together a few facts, but there seems to be very little advice / help for the interested but ignorant newcomer. I live in an area of SE Hampshire with a high percentage of Polish workers plus a large number of refugees and asylum seekers, so I assumed there would be a need for training courses and somewhere to go for advice. I find that I am on a level with the Polish workers, i.e. confused, short of friendly assistance, and in some cases having no idea where to go for aid. This is not good! ... At the moment I'm having trouble even finding a contact number for our local Immigrant Holding Centre not a mile away – God knows how strangers to the area cope with all this ridiculous and unnecessary fiddling about.'* (Email to the inquiry)

7.21   A key issue affecting the availability of places is that the available funding, whether from HEFCE (Higher Education Funding Council for England) in HEIs, or the LSC for awarding body courses, does not cover the full cost of running courses. A survey carried out in London showed that core LSC funding covered approximately 50 per cent of the cost of training a new ESOL teacher. The cost of the taught sessions was covered, but not the cost of providing teaching placements with specialist placement tutors or mentors. This is an important omission given that research shows that high-quality teaching practice placements with effective mentoring arrangements are one of the most significant elements in promoting learning progress for trainee teachers, and that the quality of this provision is patchy (Derrick, 2006; Derrick and Dicks, 2005). (This is also a problem in other curriculum areas.) **We recommend that HEFCE and the LSC should consider the level at which they are prepared to fund ESOL teacher training, to ensure that the new qualifications include high-quality teaching practice placements in a range of learning contexts, with support from ESOL specialist teacher trainers and mentors.**

7.22   There is also inconsistency in the allocation of LEA maintenance grants for learners, with the result that some in-service and new trainee teachers have to self-finance their training whereas others receive grants, bursaries or employer contributions. The current arrangements are being replaced in September

2006 by a new range of support measures: it is important that these are clear and transparent to potential learners and perceived as equitable. We welcome the intention to expand LLUK's National Reference Point to provide a point of contact and information on the available training and support. **We recommend that guidelines to LEAs on means-tested maintenance grants and funding guidelines for teachers taking ESOL teacher-training courses should be clarified.** In addition, there is varying practice among employers in the provision of remission and paid study leave. It is clearly important the release is provided for teachers studying for specialist qualifications as well as for the Certificate in FE Teaching. Clearly these are difficult considerations for small employers in particular, which suggests that there needs to be further consideration of more flexible ways of training teachers including more distance and blended learning opportunities.

Leadership and management

We have described a complex area of provision: well-informed and focused management in providers, based on good teaching and learning strategies, will be essential to successful delivery. CPD for college managers on ESOL issues will be important and ESOL should be specifically addressed in the national quality improvement strategy for Skills for Life.

8.1　It will be clear from what has been said so far in this report that ESOL is a very complex area, in terms of the heterogeneity of the learners and the difficulty of the associated pedagogy. These factors underlie the challenge for managers of ensuring that they offer diverse provision to meet multiple needs that is of consistently high quality. This challenge is compounded by the practical issue of securing enough qualified teachers. For all these reasons, effective leadership and management at middle and senior levels in provider organisations are particularly important for the ESOL portfolio. How effective are they at present?

8.2　The evidence from Ofsted and ALI inspections is that leadership and management are generally satisfactory. Day-to-day management is satisfactory but senior managers' strategy for ESOL and understanding of it are often poorly developed. In ACL settings the ESOL expertise of staff and managers is generally satisfactory but it is weaker in other areas of provision, in particular work-based training and custodial settings. Arrangements to improve quality, including the use of data, are often unsatisfactory. Promotion of equality of opportunity is satisfactory or better.

8.3　These conclusions from the inspectorates are largely mirrored by the responses to our questionnaire and the comments on our interim report, although it is worth noting that in neither context did we have more than a handful of responses from senior managers in the college context. Some respondents expressed anxiety about the extent to which the specific characteristics of ESOL and ESOL learners were fully appreciated by managers. There were concerns that ESOL was submerged in whole college procedures and approaches which had not been adapted to make them appropriate for ESOL learners. There was much consensus about the main elements of a vision of what excellent ESOL provision would look like (reflected in section 6). Respondents saw strong leadership and management at all levels as an essential element in successful provision.

8.4　The key characteristics of such leadership and management in the college context which could also be applied in other organisations include:

- clear understanding of and commitment to ESOL from senior management reflected in cross-college commitment and 'whole organisational approaches' to it, underpinned by an awareness of the education and other policy contexts in which ESOL operates and by an understanding of the circumstances in which ESOL learners live and work and how these affect learning
- middle management with direct responsibility for ESOL with good understanding of ESOL
- commitment to high quality teaching and continuous improvement, underpinned by well-resourced and effective CPD and observation of teaching and learning

- clear links between ESOL and college policies on equality and diversity
- a high status for ESOL within the college
- effort put into building effective partnerships with other providers to meet the needs of the full range of learners.

A successful strategy for ESOL will also include clearly identified pathways for learners to progress, whether within the organisation or elsewhere. Underpinning all this there has to be in place a teaching and learning strategy for ESOL which deals not only with specific ESOL provision but also with embedded ESOL and the support arrangements for ESOL learners. That strategy has to be owned and implemented by the most senior management as well as by those directly responsible for ESOL provision.

8.5 A number of respondents expressed concerns as to whether this vision was fully implemented. Concerns included the difficulty of developing a genuinely cross-college view of ESOL, particularly important in view of the relevance of ESOL issues in vocational contexts; and a concern that policy tended to be reactive to *Skills for Life* priorities and funding availability rather than responsive to learner needs.

8.6 There was no consensus about the most appropriate organisational structure to achieve these objectives, and it is not surprising that there is no single approach, given the variety of settings in which ESOL is delivered. Some respondents to our consultation argued that it should be managed separately from other provision; some thought the link with *Skills for Life* was appropriate; still others argued for a link with modern foreign languages. In practice the essential requirement is for clear and coherent management structures which address the issues set out in paragraph 8.3. The question of departmental affiliation or line management structures is less important.

8.7 Underlying the question of how ESOL is dealt with in senior management structures is an issue to which we have already referred: the lack of a clear career structure for ESOL teachers and the prevalence of part-time and temporary jobs. This inevitably means that few ESOL specialists get the opportunity to progress into management. This makes it all the more important that those responsible for ESOL have the opportunity for CPD to enable them to understand the distinctive characteristics of ESOL and the particular issues that it raises. Without such an appreciation there is a danger that the complex issues set out in this report will not be effectively addressed. There may be scope for specialist bodies in the ESOL area to consider ways in which they can contribute to the professional development of college management and other managers of ESOL provision. **We recommend that the Centre for Excellence in Leadership (CEL) should undertake work on the professional development relating to ESOL for college managers at all levels.**

This should pay particular attention to strategic planning.

8.8 We note with some surprise that there appears to have been no independent evaluation of the effectiveness of the very considerable sums of public money which have been spent on the *Skills for Life* Quality Initiative (SfLQI). In these circumstances it is difficult to see whether there are any relevant implications for the leadership and management ESOL. But **we recommend that**, in line with the thrust of several of the other recommendations in this report, **ESOL should be more specifically addressed in the national quality improvement strategy for *Skills for Life*, funded by the QIA.** The work we have proposed should be undertaken by CEL will be important in this context.

Funding

9

We argue that the current funding arrangements cannot be sustained in the long term given the increasing pressures of demand. But it would be wrong, in terms both of equity and policy objectives, to offer lesser entitlements to ESOL learners as compared to other Skills for Life learners. We recommend a series of changes to current funding arrangements designed to focus funding better on the most needy, and recommend a changed set of funding entitlements for the longer term.

9.1   Funding is inevitably one of the main topics which the Committee has discussed and was raised by almost all the respondents to our consultation. There is no doubt that very substantial public resources have been devoted to ESOL: £279 million from the LSC in 2004–5. Despite that level of resource (and the LSC is only one, albeit the largest, of the funders of ESOL) there is, as we have already noted, a substantial amount of unmet demand in the system from learners, and there are pressures on the funding of teacher training and CPD. But it would be foolish simply to note this and recommend an increase in public funding. Such a recommendation would be unrealistic in the context of current pressures on expenditure and would not recognise that the state is not the only source or potential source of funding. Neither would it allow some of the important infrastructure and policy issues which we have identified to be addressed. Rather we need to consider whether the current funding arrangements are working effectively in directing resource to where it is most needed, whether current arrangements have any unintended consequences and whether the overall effect of funding is to support appropriate policy objectives. We have to address all these issues satisfactorily before considering whether there is a case for increased funding.

9.2   We have argued above that effective ESOL provision is key to a number of policy agendas: it underpins not only education and skills objectives but also important objectives in relation to social cohesion, citizenship and regeneration. It is reasonable to expect that the funds devoted to those policy areas should contribute to the cost of ESOL provision where it supports their key objectives, and this should be one of the outcomes of our first recommendation. To some extent, this is already the case. There is a bewildering variety of funding sources for ESOL provision, each with its own eligibility rules, output targets, quality measures and reporting requirements. Inevitably this produces confusion for both providers and learners and produces substantial management and administrative overheads for providers. This is a particular issue for organisations in the voluntary and community sector which do not always have the resources to cope with these demands and which have great difficulty in securing stable core funding. The variety of funding sources and of providers also raises important issues about the planning of provision at both national and local levels, and we return to this issue below.

9.3   It is difficult to believe that the current funding arrangements are the most effective way of meeting the needs of current ESOL learners and potential learners or of delivering the key policy objectives to which ESOL provision contributes. Much of the evidence submitted to our inquiry suggests that current arrangements do not always direct funding to the learners who most need it. This is hardly surprising since current funding comes from multiple sources, which have been developed at different times and with different priorities, while the major source of funding, from the *Skills for Life* initiative, has to a considerable extent been driven by the objectives and the priorities of basic literacy and numeracy rather than the specific needs of ESOL learners. It is essential that these issues are addressed in any review of the funding for ESOL.

9.4   As noted above, there is a wide variety of funding sources for ESOL in addition to LSC mainstream funding. This is an inevitable consequence of the variety of ESOL learners and their varying needs, and of the centrality of language needs to learners' wider concerns. We have discussed JCP funding in section 5. Particular concerns raised with us about the other funding streams involved include the following:

- *ACL funding*[26] (also from the LSC) is valued because it provides the opportunity to make provision for groups who do not want or need accreditation for their learning, for example elderly people, and because it provides the opportunity to make provision for vulnerable groups not eligible for other funding. But there are concerns that the signs are that ACL funding will decrease over the next few years.
- *European Union funding* (European Social Fund and EQUAL) and *Single Regeneration Budget (SRB)* are valued because they are flexible funding sources which can be used for innovative provision and work with disadvantaged groups not eligible for mainstream funding. But these funding sources are subject to complex reporting requirements and bureaucracy, and are thus demanding of management time (not always available to smaller organisations in the voluntary and community sector). They are also time limited, presenting problems of sustainability and continuity. However, the flexibility of ESF programmes has been helpful in ensuring the social inclusion and increased employability of many ESOL learners. It would be helpful if ESOL were to have a higher profile in future ESF advice.
- *Employer Training Pilots (ETP)* were valued by the few ESOL providers who had accessed this funding during the pilots because it could be used to pay for short courses. However, the downside is that for ESOL learners there were insufficient hours to make real progress, and there were concerns that the management overheads of the programme are disproportionate. With the roll-out of Train to Gain, we have, as we noted in para 5.16, serious doubts whether the design and policy intentions of the Train to Gain programme are appropriate to the needs of ESOL learners.
- *Key characteristics of funding arrangements.*

9.5   It is not within the scope of this Committee to devise a detailed set of proposals for the funding of ESOL. Nor do we have the resources to cost precisely the impact of current levels of demand or of the proposals we make below. But from our work we can identify some of the key priorities which we believe ESOL funding should address and some of the key elements we believe should characterise the funding arrangements. We hope this will be helpful to those responsible for policy in this area.

9.6   We believe that effective funding arrangements for ESOL should:

- ensure that free provision is targeted to ensure that the adults most at risk of social exclusion benefit
- ensure that sufficient appropriate ESOL provision is available for all adults who need it
- be as simple as possible, easy to understand and to manage. In particular, it is essential that there are clear entitlements for individuals which are easy to understand and to validate. We discuss below what those entitlements might be
- have the capacity to support a wide variety of providers. In particular voluntary and community groups, including small organisations, should be able to access funding to help reach some of the hardest to help potential learners
- support a wider variety of provision than currently. In particular, funding arrangements should be capable of providing support for ESOL which is embedded in vocational courses; for employment-related provision; for more intensive courses, particularly for new arrivals; and for learning at Level 3 and above. The aim should be that each location (perhaps best defined in terms of LSC areas) should have the right balance of provision to meet the full range of identified ESOL needs in the area
- be available in both urban and rural areas
- not put undue burdens on either learners or providers.

---

[26] Adult and Community Learning, part of which is now referred to as Personal and Community Development Learning in recent White Papers.

9.7   Some of the cost of providing ESOL will be met by public funds, but we also argue below that there are circumstances in which it would be right to look for contributions from individuals and employers. However, there is a clear policy requirement to ensure that the arrangements taken together will meet identified ESOL needs and the requirements outlined above.

Current arrangements

9.8   Under current arrangements, the government funds free ESOL for the following groups:

- eligible adults, whether migrants or members of settled communities, who do not have English language skills up to Level 2. This includes people receiving Jobseeker's Allowance who register for one of the New Deals and are assessed to have English language needs. This funding is offered as part of the wider *Skills for Life* strategy, a fact which we argue below has some unfortunate, and presumably unintended, consequences for ESOL provision
- all asylum seekers and refugees on arrival in the UK.

We assume that the *Skills for Life* strategy will be maintained until at least the end of the PSA period in 2010 and that ESOL at Level 2 and below will remain a part of the strategy. In the immediate future there is a particular issue about the entitlements to free learning available to ESOL learners and those available to literacy and numeracy learners. Free provision for all eligible learners below Level 2 might not sustainable in the long term without additional funding, but it would be unacceptable to remove that entitlement from ESOL learners while retaining it for literacy and numeracy. Such a course of action would be unfair and discriminatory. For the same reasons it would not be right to introduce a means-tested regime for ESOL learners alone. But when the system of entitlements for literacy and numeracy learners is reviewed it would be right to review it for ESOL learners too.

We turn now to consider the implications for some of the current funding streams, both in the short term until new entitlements can be introduced and for the longer term.

Immediate funding issues

9.9   By far the major source of funding for ESOL work is the LSC. There is no doubt that ESOL funding from the LSC has substantially increased over the past few years. It benefits automatically from the basic skills uplift, and in addition there is a disadvantage uplift of 12 per cent. Compared to other areas of the curriculum ESOL has positive relative weightings and a well-funded package of resource. ESOL enrolments increased from 296,899 in 2001–2 to 454,541 in 2003–4 and funding from £170 million to £256 million over the same period (KPMG, 2005). It benefits from the priority accorded to *Skills for Life* provision within LSC planning. All this is positive for ESOL, and is widely welcomed by practitioners.

9.10   There is an important issue about the *relationship between EFL and ESOL* qualifications. The LSC does not fund EFL qualifications for free provision, and when the new rules came into effect some provision was moved from EFL to ESOL as the latter was the only available source of funding. As a consequence, some learners who would previously have undertaken EFL courses, and paid for their learning, now take free ESOL courses. The LSC understandably wishes to address this issue, and to ensure that where it is clear, following assessment, that learners require EFL provision, they should be placed on appropriate full-cost courses leading to EFL qualifications. But, as we have noted earlier in this report, the distinction between ESOL and EFL is much less clear than in the past and there is a real danger that reliance on an outmoded distinction will result in a system where the provision that a learner undertakes is the result of their ability to pay rather than their learning needs. It is essential that we do not produce a funding system which in effect denies access to appropriate provision to people who are not able to pay. For some of these learners provision which would be categorised as EFL will be appropriate. That is why we have recommended revisions to the funding system which would base entitlement on learners' circumstances and learning goals rather than on a categorisation of types of provision.

9.11 We have received a number of comments about the *impact of targets* on funding. The new ESOL qualifications are the only nationally approved ESOL qualifications eligible for funding. LSC (2006) guidance is that Entry 1 and Entry 2 provision which leads to qualifications is fundable. The LSC aims for providers to shift the majority of their provision to programmes offering eligible qualifications, and has set a benchmark of 80 per cent of learners working towards nationally approved qualifications and 20 per cent not. The 20 per cent will include provision below Entry Level 1 and learners not enrolled on an approved qualification.

9.12 It seems clear that Entry 1 and Entry 2 provision which leads to qualifications is fundable. But in many local areas LSCs are in effect prioritising provision which counts towards the LSC's PSA targets which are expressed in terms of nationally approved qualifications at Entry Level 3 and Levels 1 and 2. It is not clear whether this is a consequence of the LSCs themselves choosing to fund only provision which counts towards PSA targets, or whether providers are in effect anticipating this. But the consequence is that in many parts of the country it is difficult to get sufficient funding to meet demand for Pre-Entry level and Entry Levels 1 and 2 provision which is urgently needed by learners, and that in those areas the portfolio of ESOL provision is unbalanced. Even in terms of current policy priorities this seems an irrational approach. Learners who are unable to acquire language skills at these levels will find it much more difficult to enter or progress within the workforce and even the most basic jobs require basic language skills. The research evidence is that the transition from Entry 2 to Entry 3 in literacy has the greatest impact on learners' life chances, and this is likely to be equally true for language learners (Bynner and Parsons, 2005). A failure to fund provision at these levels may also make it much more difficult to provide appropriate progression routes for learners who start in community-based or ACL settings and aim to progress into college courses (which would be relevant to the PSA targets). It would be helpful to introduce a sub-target at Entry Level 2 to ensure that these learners are not overlooked when provision is planned. **We recommend that the guidance to local LSCs should make it clear that Entry Level 1 and 2 provision leading to nationally approved qualifications is fundable, that a sub-target for Entry Level 2 should be introduced and that one of the objectives of their purchasing strategy for ESOL should be to achieve a balanced portfolio of provision with clear progression routes available for learners.**

9.13 A further area of concern is that only the full ESOL *Skills for Life* certificate counts towards the targets. As noted above, practitioners have warmly welcomed the unit-based structure of the new qualifications and consider that they meet the needs of learners. However, the qualification guidelines recommend 100 guided learning hours for each mode, and some learners take longer. In practice many learners will only be able to achieve one mode during a year and thus will not count against the targets as having a full achievement. Again this is likely to have a distorting effect on provision. It is also inequitable that the *Skills for Life* literacy exam does count towards the targets while the reading mode of the ESOL certificate, which is identical, does not. Furthermore, the speaking and listening unit of an ESOL qualification is sufficient for application for UK citizenship. To free up provision for would-be citizens, LSC should fund the accreditation which the government requires applicants to achieve

9.14 Another consequence of the current targets is that it is increasingly difficult to get funding for provision at Levels 3 and above. This has a particular impact on refugees and asylum seekers who need higher-level language qualifications to be able to enter employment in their existing professions. There is a particular demand for IELTS qualifications because they are required for entry to employment and HE. These qualifications are not fundable under LSC *Skills for Life* funding, and alternative funding sources are difficult to find, although for the next year IELTS 6/7 and Cambridge Proficiency will be funded by the LSC at national base rate. We have recommended an approach to funding this provision which would rely on contributions from individuals and employers. But the loan scheme we recommend would require some underpinning from public funds, and we believe that major public sectors which rely on skilled migrants should bear some of the costs of their acquisition of language skills.

9.15   Many providers express concern that the difficulties noted above are likely to be exacerbated as resources are squeezed further and the pressure is increased on the 80/20 benchmark and the PSA targets. Learner support such as childcare and help with transport costs will be even more difficult to fund. Rationing is already in place in many areas, through shortening programmes, offering only part-time programmes and excluding learners whose pattern of attendance is erratic. There is also concern that very short courses are no longer funded: this affects initial and diagnostic provision, with the effect that learners may be directed to inappropriate courses with an adverse impact on retention and achievement. What we would like to see is some clear expectation that initial and diagnostic assessment is properly done for all ESOL learners and that funding arrangements encourage this. Such a steer could be given through special arrangements for a three-hour funded short course and as part of the 1.4 uplift. The short course funding was originally withdrawn because it did not appear to directly benefit learners in many cases. However, the LSC retained the right to fund specific short programmes of assessment where necessary. Concern remains that newly-arrived family members will continue to be excluded from LSC-funded provision despite the negative impact this will have on settlement. At least one major national provider expects to drop ESOL provision because it will become uneconomic as the new funding rules tighten. This presents a bleak prospect for ESOL learners for the future.

9.16   We have noted above that ESOL provision is currently well resourced compared to other areas of provision, in recognition of the disadvantage suffered by many learners and the expensive nature of much provision. But there are still many potential learners (often women) who are only ready or able to participate in provision provided in informal settings close to their homes: such provision is expensive and difficult to run. It is often difficult to find appropriate funding for other initiatives to widen participation and improve quality, and for development work, and such funding as is available is usually time limited and often beset with complex reporting arrangements and sometimes with inappropriate targets. We believe that it is important to make resources available to support innovative work aimed at the most disadvantaged groups.

Impact on key learner groups

9.17   We believe that the only equitable and practicable approach is to treat EU migrants in the same way as settled communities. It has been argued that much of the current pressure on ESOL funding is the consequence of increased migration from the A8 countries and that because many of these migrants do not intend to settle in the long term they should not be entitled to free ESOL provision. In fact, there were waiting lists for ESOL provision in London for many years before the A8 migration. Quite apart from the dubious legality of a proposition to treat these EU citizens differently from settled communities, we think it would be wrong in principle to proceed in this way. These migrants are performing essential tasks, often attracted here by employers seeking to address labour shortages. Helping them improve their English language skills will make them more effective employees and assist them to integrate and contribute to their communities more effectively, improving social cohesion in the areas in which they have settled. There is also the practical difficulty of testing intentions: it will not take long before it is well known that the way to get free ESOL provision is to say that you intend to remain in the UK long term. Another concern is that if a charge were made for ESOL while literacy remained free, some ESOL learners would migrate to free literacy provision that is inappropriate for their needs.

9.18   We understand that active consideration is being given to the removal of the entitlement of asylum seekers to free ESOL. Even if the rationale for this is to cease free provision for people who may not be entitled to stay in the long term, this seems a harsh measure given the circumstances of many of those who would be affected. When asylum seekers arrive they need to learn English if only to survive for the time that the Home Office takes to make a decision. We note that the New Asylum Model means that decision should be taken on applications for asylum within eight weeks. Given the very difficult personal circumstances of the great majority of asylum seekers and the research evidence that language learning is much more effective if offered soon after arrival, asylum seekers should become entitled to ESOL provision when the target period for decisions in asylum applications ends, whether or not a decision has been taken in an individual case. **We recommend that if the immediate entitlement of asylum seekers to free ESOL provision is withdrawn, asylum seekers should have the same entitlements as home learners when the target period for decision on their application has expired.**

9.19 There is a particular issue about the newly-arrived *spouses and family members of permanent UK residents*. At present spouses or fiancées of permanent UK residents are allowed access to free ESOL only after one year, and other family members after three years. The great majority of these people will be intending, and entitled to, permanent settlement. Improving their language skills will be of immense benefit in helping them integrate into the UK, improve the chances of their becoming economically active and reducing reliance on benefits, and thus help improve social cohesion. It is difficult to see any logical explanation for the current policy, and it is unfair to a vulnerable group. **We therefore recommend that spouses, fiancées and family members of permanent UK residents should have immediate access to the same entitlements to ESOL provision as permanent residents.**

9.20 We recognise that there are serious issues about the funding of ESOL and how best to prioritise amongst the many pressing current needs. As we note above, we believe that the scope for radically changing the funding system is limited until the wider system applying to *Skills for Life* is changed. But we believe that the immediate adjustments we have proposed in this section will help focus resources where they are most needed and, for the longer term, we believe that the recommended approach will both target scarce resource where it will have most impact and help address the current issues of capacity.

Future funding arrangements

9.21 More radical changes are needed to ensure that a sustainable approach is developed to offer accessible and affordable ESOL to those who need it. Our recommendations in this section aim to ensure that free ESOL is targeted to the adults most at risk of exclusion, but that sufficient paid-for ESOL is available to meet the needs of all who need it to enable them to live and work in the UK. Our assumption is that this will not be free to all, but that some supplementary funding would be required, either from individuals themselves or from their employers, to take new learners of English up to Level 2 and beyond.

9.22 We have carefully considered whether an entitlement to 500 hours' free learning for learners with language skills below Level 2 would be an appropriate approach. The most common approach to entitlements to language provision in other EU countries and some other major anglophone countries is to offer new arrivals entitlement to a number of hours of free tuition, most commonly 500 hours.[27] It is important to note that this entitlement, if applied in the UK context, would not in itself be sufficient to take a new arrival from having no language to Level 2 competence, which is the base for further study or full effectiveness at work and in the community. The actual number of hours needed by each learner is difficult to quantify as rates of progress differ. The best estimate is that some 1000–1500 hours are required for that learning journey, although recent research suggests there is clear evidence that experiential learning outside the classroom is just as, if not more, valuable than learning in the classroom (Baynham *et al*., forthcoming). This means that the number of funded learning hours required, although considerable, might be less.

---

[27] See Annexe 3

9.23 Whilst this approach has merit, we believe it would be very difficult to introduce such an entitlement when literacy and numeracy learners are entitled to free provision up to Level 2. In effect the rules would discriminate against ESOL learners, many of whom will be members of settled communities. There is a real danger that such a provision could be challenged as racist. Whilst free provision up to Level 2 is available to *Skills for Life* learners, it should be available to ESOL learners too. But we recognise that there is a case for re-examining the position when the commitment to free *Skills for Life* provision is reviewed, presumably at the end of the PSA period in 2010. From that point it would be appropriate to have a more focused approach.

9.24 We believe that ESOL entitlement should be as follows:

- All adults with English language learning needs should have a right to a free assessment of up to three hours.
- All ESOL learners with language skills below Level 1 should be entitled to free provision until they have reached that level.
- Above Level 1, provision should be paid for at vocational rates, with an effective remissions system to ensure that those in financial need can still access provision.

9.25 Adults with language skills below Level 1 are likely to experience the most difficulty in participating in their communities, accessing services and securing employment and progressions at work. Helping these people engage in their communities and to give them the skills they need to progress in learning and at work is essential both for them as individuals and for the government's wider policies on integration and cohesion. These factors support offering free provision up to Level 1 for those with ESOL needs. **We therefore recommend that when the current *Skills for Life* entitlements are revised, all ESOL learners with language skills below Level 1 should be entitled to free provision until they have reached that level.** Above that level provision should be subject to fees. However, ability to pay is a particular concern for adults on benefits, low wages, and women with home and caring responsibilities who are not earning, or whose learning needs might not be considered a priority in the home, so there must be a robust remissions system to ensure that those in greatest need continue to have access to provision. The Committee felt strongly that the good work undertaken through family learning and family LLN programmes should be developed (see paragraphs 4.10–4.16). It was felt that an increase in family ESOL programmes was needed and this would encourage women who were under-represented in English language programmes, such as those from Bangladeshi and Pakistani communities, to obtain greater skills.[28] **We recommend an increase to the LSC's Personal and Community Development budget to support an increase in family ESOL programmes, aimed specifically at increasing opportunities for women from under-represented ethnic minority communities.**

9.26 The Committee is convinced by the arguments put to us by teachers and researchers that initial and diagnostic assessment is fundamental to placing learners on the right programme. It would be essential to ensure that all potential ESOL learners have a thorough assessment of their needs before deciding on an appropriate learning path. **We recommend that all people with ESOL requirements should have the right to a free initial assessment of up to three hours.**

Funding beyond Level 1

9.27 In line with our concern to ensure that ESOL is funded and targeted to ensure the inclusion of excluded adults with the most complex circumstances, it follows that the 1.4 funding uplift should be also be

---

[28] Pakistanis and Bangladeshis have the lowest level of English language proficiency of all the major ethnic minority groups: '…only four per cent of Bangladeshi and 28 per cent of Pakistani women aged 45–64 years spoke English fluently or well. Fluency in English has been found to increase people's probability of being employed by up to 25 per cent' (Tackey, N.D. *et al.*, 2006).

targeted to support inclusion of these learners. In other words, for provision that incurs additional costs for inclusion strategies such as small group sizes and high quality locally sited provision. Some supplementary funding would also be required, either from individuals themselves or from their employers, to take new learners of English to Level 2 and beyond.

9.28   Learners in the focus groups which we convened for this inquiry were not in general hostile to the principle that they should contribute to the cost of their course, but were, of course, anxious about their ability to do so. Many of the client group for ESOL, if in work at all, are in low-paid work and often support families overseas as well as in the UK. The ability to pay was a particular concern for adults on benefits, low wages, and women with home and caring responsibilities who were not earning, or whose learning needs might not be considered a priority in the home. Whilst many of these adults will be eligible for fee remission, others will not be eligible but still struggle to find fees. **We recommend that the government should explore the development of a subsidised loan scheme for individuals not entitled to further free provision or fee remission who wish to undertake ESOL learning beyond their basic entitlement, especially for higher-level learning.**

9.29   So far as employers are concerned, we have argued above that employers derive significant benefits from improved language skills among the migrant workers whom they attract to work in the UK. It will clearly be important to ensure that employers are engaged through their SSCs in addressing the English language development needs of their workforces. The extent of engagement will depend on whether ESOL appears as an issue in the relevant Sector Skills Agreement, which in turn depends on whether it has been raised by those preparing the Agreement. We were disturbed to discover that ESOL has not been raised in all Sector Skills Agreement discussions. We welcome the coordinating role of Asset Skills for the SSCs: we hope that they will be able to work on raising awareness among employers generally of the importance of ESOL to work and in considering ways in which employers might contribute to English language provision. Evidence from the ESOL Pathfinder projects suggests that it is likely that some employers could be persuaded of the economic arguments for investing in ESOL training. Similarly some Union Learning Fund projects have successfully engaged employers in contributing to the costs of ESOL training for their workforce. But the Pathfinder projects also showed that employers whose general employment practices were poor were reluctant to pay for staff training. Just as we have recommended that A-rated employers of non-EU migrant workers should be required to fund ESOL provision for their workers (paragraph 3.25) **we recommend that the Department of Trade and Industry (DTI) should make it a condition of granting licences to employment agencies recruiting from EU countries that they should, at their expense, ensure that their workers are enabled to secure adequate English language skills, whether in their country of origin or in the UK.** More generally, we believe that employers should be encouraged to help their employees, whether from migrant or settled communities, to secure adequate English language skills. **We therefore recommend that the government should ensure that employers secure ESOL provision for their workers, whether from migrant or settled communities. To support the measures recommended in paragraphs 3.25 and 9.29 it is crucial that regulatory and enforcement measures are adopted to ensure employers are prevented from transferring costs to workers, including migrant workers, and ensure the exploitation of migrant workers does not increase.** This might include incentives linked into schemes such as Investors in People and the Chartermark (and might apply to all *Skills for Life* programmes, not just ESOL).

9.30   As we have noted earlier in this report, there are significant needs for language skills above Level 2 for those migrants with professional and high level skills, to enable them to enter HE and to use their skills in this country and thus make a full contribution to the UK's economic performance. Such courses should be funded either as vocational courses with remission for eligible learners or as full cost recovery courses. We believe that in some cases employers and potential employers should bear some of the cost of such learning. A major employer like the NHS which relies heavily on skilled migrant labour should bear some of the cost of improving its workers' language skills to the necessary level. There will also be learners who are willing themselves to invest in the necessary learning but need assistance to meet the up-front costs. This supports the argument that the loan scheme recommended in paragraph 9.28 be available at this higher level because these are the people most likely to secure well-paid jobs and be in a position to repay the loan. Employers and the state should bear the cost at lower levels.

9.31 These recommendations add up to a radical reshaping of the funding priorities and entitlements to ESOL provision, but we believe that they would produce a better targeted and more equitable system than the current arrangements. However, to test these proposals it is important that they should be properly modelled and an impact assessment carried out, particularly on their race, gender and other equal opportunities implications. This might form part of the Comprehensive Spending Review study recommended above.

What next?

10.1 The Committee was pleased to be able to launch this report in time for it to be offered to Lord Leitch as part of his review of skills for the Treasury and in time for it to assist those with responsibility for the forthcoming Comprehensive Spending Review. We are also pleased that the report could be launched at a conference addressed by the minister responsible, the Rt. Hon. Bill Rammell MP on 3rd October 2006 in Westminster.

10.2 In the previous sections we have identified many recommendations which are listed for ease of use in section 2. The Committee are unanimous in their view that ESOL must be a cross-government concern and that is why we have recommended a cross-departmental review. It is only by working together that we will see improvements made to the infrastructure which supports those who require ESOL provision. As the lead department for ESOL, the DfES has been active in our Committee and we have ensured that all our deliberations have been shared with both the DfES and the LSC as we have gone along.

10.3 Our report only relates to England. The Scottish Executive have shared their views with us and are producing their own ESOL Strategy for Scotland. The Committee looks forward with interest to see how the other UK countries manage their ESOL arrangements and would be pleased to offer advice and support on ESOL where it may be helpful.

10.4 The report is offered to the DfES as a contribution to the challenges facing the Department in relation to future funding of learning and skills. At about the time the Committee was established the Secretary of State requested advice from the LSC on ESOL through the annual grant letter to the Council. This report is a contribution to the LSC's work in response to that request.

10.5 Our key recommendations include the setting up of regional planning fora and a ministerial lead, a review of how ESOL is implemented, and the creation of an advisory group or forum on ESOL to act as a source of advice and expertise. We think these kinds of actions will encourage confidence among providers and teachers and enable the many challenges in ESOL provision to be addressed in a considered and effective way.

10.6 NIACE and partners will be seeking wider discussion of the report, its recommendations and findings, through national and regional conferences, articles in professional journals, and in the press and media. Committee members have agreed at their final meeting to consider progress in September 2007. That way we will be able to consider and then report on progress one year on. During the year NIACE will continue its advocacy of ESOL programmes and those who need them.

10.7 We have not costed our recommendations but believe that any savings made through changes in the funding rules should be re-invested in ESOL, on those in greatest potential need. This includes learners at lowest achievement levels, those in the poorest communities and learners for whom ESOL is a bridge to citizenship, employment and social inclusion.

References

ALI (2004a) *Annual Report of the Chief Inspector 2003–04*. London: Adult Learning Inspectorate.

ALI (2004b) *Basic Skills for Offenders in the Community*. London: Adult Learning Inspectorate.

ALI (2005) *Annual Report of the Chief Inspector 2004–05*. London: Adult Learning Inspectorate.

Barton, D. and Pitt, K. (2003) *Adult ESOL Pedagogy: A Review of Research, An Annotated Bibliography and Recommendations for Future Research*. London: NRDC.

Baynham, M., Roberts, C., Cooke, M., Simpson, J. and Ananiadou, K. *The ESOL Effective Practice Project,* London: NRDC, forthcoming.

Bloch, A. (2002) *Refugees' Opportunities and Barriers in Employment and Training (DWP Research report)*.

Braggins, J. and Talbot, J. (2003) *Time to Learn. Prisoners' Views on Prison Education*. London: Prison Reform Trust.

Bynner, J. and Parsons, S. (2005) *New Light on Literacy and Numeracy: Results of the Literacy and Numeracy Assessment in the Age 34 Follow-Up of the 1970 Cohort Study* (BCS70). London: NRDC, University of London.

Crick, B. (2006) 'Language games', *Prospect*, July, p. 16.

Dalziel, D. and Sofres, T.N. (2005) *ESOL Pathfinder Learners' Survey and Prisons Report*. London: Department for Education and Skills.

Derrick J. (2006) 'Improving the quality of teaching practice placements on pre-service initial teacher training programmes', *Basic Skills Professional Development,* 6, pp. 8–10.

Derrick, J. and Dicks, J. (2005) *Teaching Practice and Mentoring: The Key to Effective Literacy, Language and Numeracy Teacher Training*. Leicester: NIACE.

DfEE (1998) *The Learning Age*. London: Department for Education and Employment.

DfEE (2000) *Breaking the Language Barriers: The Report of the Working Group on English for Speakers of Other Languages*. London: Department for Education and Employment.

DfES (2002) *Success for All*. London: Department for Education and Skills.

DfES (2003a) *Planning Learning and Recording Progress and Achievement*. London: Department for Education and Skills.

DfES (2003b) *The Skills for Life Teaching Qualifications Framework: A User's Guide*. Department for Education and Skills.

DfES (2004) *Equipping our Teachers for the Future: Reforming Initial Teacher Training for the Learning and Skills Sector.* London: Department for Education and Skills.

DfES (2005a) *Extended Schools: Access to Services and Opportunities for All. A Prospectus*. London: Department for Education and Skills.

DfES (2005b) *Offender Learning Green Paper: Reducing Re-offending through Skills and Employment*. At: http://www.dfes.gov.uk/offenderlearning/index.cfm?fuseaction=content.view&CategoryID=3&ContentID=11

DfES (2005c) *The Offender's Learning Journey*. London: Department for Education and Skills.

DfES (2005d) *Skills for Communities*. London: Department for Education and Skills.

DfES (2006a) *ESOL Access for All: Guidance on Making the Adult ESOL Curriculum Accessible. Part 1*. London: Department for Education and Skills.

DfES (2006b) *Further Education: Raising Skills, Improving Life Chances.* London: Department for Education and Skills.

DfES/FENTO (2002) *Subject Specifications for Teachers of English for Speakers of Other Languages (ESOL)*.

Dumper, H. (2002) *Is it Safe Here? Refugee Women's Experiences in the UK*. London: Refugee Action.

Dustmann, C. and Fabbri, F. (2003) 'Language proficiency and labour market performance of immigrants in the UK', *The Economic Journal*, 113(489), pp. 695–717.

DWP (2005) *Working to Rebuild Lives. A Refugee Employment Strategy*. London: Department of Work and Pensions.

Eldred, J., Ward, J., Snowden, K. and Dutton, Y. (2005) *Catching Confidence: The Nature and Role of Confidence – Ways of Recording Changes in the Learning Context*. Leicester: NIACE.

Gilpin, N., Henty, M., Lemos, S., Portes, J. and Bullen, C. (2006) *The Impact of Free Movement of Workers from Central and Eastern Europe on the UK Labour Market*. DWP working paper no. 29. London: Department for Work and Pensions.

Gregory, E. (1996) 'Learning from the community: A family literacy project with Bangladeshi-origin children in London', in S. Wolfendale and K. Topping (eds) *Family Involvement in Literacy*. London: Cassell.

HM Government (2004) *Every Child Matters: Change for Children*. London: Department for Education and Skills. At: http://www.everychildmatters.gov.uk

Home Office (2001) *Community Cohesion: A Report of the Independent Review Team Chaired by Ted Cantle*. London: Home Office.

Home Office (2005a) *Improving Opportunity, Strengthening Society: The Government's Strategy to Increase Race Equality and Community Cohesion*. London: Home Office.

Home Office (2005b) *Integration Matters: A National Strategy for Refugee Integration*. London: Home Office.

Home Office (2006) *A Five Year Strategy for Protecting the Public and Reducing Re-offending*. Cm 6717. London: Home Office.

References

Kirk, R. (2004) *Skills Audit of Refugees*. Home Office online report 37/04. At: http://www.homeoffice.gov.uk/rds/pdfs04/rdsolr3704.pdf

Kofman, E., Raghuram, P. and Merefield, M. (2005) *Gendered Migrations: Towards Gender Sensitive Policies in the UK*. London: Institute for Public Policy Research.

KPMG (2005) *Review of English for Speakers of Other Languages*. London: Department for Education and Skills/Learning and Skills Council.

Leitch, S. (2005) *Skills in the UK: The Long-Term Challenge*. At: http://www.hm-treasury.gov.uk/independent_reviews/leitch_review/review_leitch_index.cfm

LSC (2006) *Policy Requirements for Planning: Managing the Balance and Mix of Provision*. Coventry: Learning and Skills Council.

Lyons, M. (2006) *National Prosperity, Local Choice and Civic Engagement: A New Partnership between Central and Local Government for the 21st Century*. At: http://www.lyonsinquiry.org.uk/docs/

Mallows, D. (2006) *Review of NRDC Research in ESOL*. London: NRDC, forthcoming.

Moser, C. (1999) *A Fresh Start: Improving Literacy and Numeracy*. London: Department for Education and Employment.

ODPM (2005) *Improving Services, Improving Lives: Evidence and Key Themes*. London: Social Exclusion Unit.

Ofsted (2003) *The Initial Training of Further Education Teachers*. London: Ofsted.

Ofsted (2005) *Raising the Achievement of Bilingual Learners*. London: Ofsted.

Rees, S., Savitzky, F. and Malik, A. (eds) (2003) *On the Road. Journeys in Family Learning*. London: London Language and Literacy Unit

Refugee Council (2005a) *Making Women Visible: Strategies for a More Woman-Centred Asylum and Refugee Support System*. London: Refugee Council. At: http://www.refugeecouncil.org.uk/policy/responses/2005/women.htm

Refugee Council (2005b) *A Study of Asylum Seekers with Special Needs*. London: Refugee Council. At: http://www.refugeecouncil.org.uk/policy/position/2005/specialneeds.htm

Roberts, C. *et al*. (2004) *English for Speakers of Other Languages (ESOL): Case Studies of Provision, Learners' Needs and Resources*. London: NRDC.

Roberts, C. *et al*. (2005) *Embedded Teaching and Learning of Adult Literacy, Numeracy and ESOL*. London: NRDC.

Spiegel, M. and Sunderland, H. (2006) *Teaching Basic Literacy to ESOL Learners*. London: LLU+.

Tackey, N.D. *et al*. (2006) *Barriers to Employment for Pakistanis and Bangladeshis in Britain*. London: Institute for Employment Studies for Department for Work and Pensions. Research report No. 360, p. 2. At: http://www.employment-studies.co.uk/pubs/report.php?id=dwp360

TUC (2003) *Overworked, Underpaid and Over Here. Migrant Workers in Britain*. London: Trades Union Congress.

Uden, T. (2004) *Learning's Not a Crime*. Leicester: NIACE.

Ward, J. and Kerwin, M. (2005) *Report of the Evaluation of the Cumbria Offenders into Learning Initiative* (unpublished).

Members of the ESOL Committee

Chair

Derek Grover CB	**Chair**

Members

Mary Alys Regional Co-ordinator TUC Learning Services	**TUC**
Jenny Burnette (From April 2006) Director for Strategic Reform and Development Quality Improvement Agency	**QIA**
Mary Clayton (Until Feb 2006) ESOL Programme Leader Thomas Danby College	**FE college practitioner**
Mary Coussey Advisory Board on Naturalisation & Integration – Chair	**Advisory Board on Naturalisation & Integration**
Sue Diplock Head of School of ESOL Waltham Forest College	**National Association for Teaching English and other Community Languages to Adults**
Paul Hambley *Skills for Life* Manager	**Lifelong Learning UK**
Paul Head Principal and Chief Exective The College of North East London	**FE college**
Dr Ursula Howard Director NRDC	**National Research and Development Centre**

Denia Kincade
(From July 2006)
Curriculum Manager for ESOL
Liverpool Community College

FE college practitioner

Jan Luff
(Until July 2006)
Curriculum Manager for ESOL
Liverpool Community College

FE college practitioner

Jackie McLoughlin MBE
Curriculum Manager ESOL
Croydon CETS

LEA ACL practitioner

Alastair Pearson
Adult Learning Inspector

Adult Learning Inspectorate

Helen Sunderland
Head of ESOL, LLU+
London South Bank University

LLU+ at London South Bank University

John Taylor
Principal and Chief Executive
Sheffield College

College

Meena Wood
HMI
Office for Standards in Education

Ofsted

Observers

Philippa Langton
Learning and Skills Council
London Region

Learning and Skills Council

Martin Norfield
Skills for Life Strategy Unit
DfES

Department for Education and Skills

Project Coordination

Dr Jane Ward

Professional Adviser – NIACE

Dr Peter Lavender OBE

Deputy Director – NIACE

Giustine Kettle

Administration – NIACE

Dr Yanina Dutton

Research Assistant – NIACE

Substitutes

Denia Kincade for Jan Luff
Pip Kings for Philippa Langton
Dina Kiwan for Mary Coussey
Andrew Oatridge for John Taylor
Sue Yeomans for Jenny Burnette

Gathering the evidence

2.1 Our approach to gathering the evidence

We used a range of approaches to gather evidence to ensure as wide a range of voices from the learners themselves as well all those connected to educational work with adult speakers of other languages in ESOL and related areas, including practitioners, managers, policy makers, funders, and inspectors. We set up an ESOL committee page on the NIACE website and there were 7580 visits and 2955 downloads of the interim report during the course of the Inquiry. In the first phase we carried out a literature survey and drew on the expertise of committee members to identify the main issues. We then gathered written and oral evidence in relation to these issues to inform our thinking and help us to formulate our recommendations to policy makers, providers, inspectorates, managers and teachers which we set out in our interim report. In the second phase we investigated a number of areas in more depth and consulted widely on the contents of the interim report.

2.2 The evidence

Research

- We carried out a survey of research studies and policy documents to identify and illuminate the major issues and challenges facing ESOL. An initial scoping paper was produced and posted on the NIACE website. This will be published as a separate document.
- We surveyed approaches to entitlements to language provision in other EU countries and major anglophone countries.[1]
- *Review of NRDC Research in ESOL*, David Mallows, NRDC.

Committee meetings

The committee held five meetings where we debated the following issues:
- Learner demand
- Policy issues
- Funding
- Effective practice and quality
- ESOL for work
- ESOL for citizenship and social justice
- Teacher recruitment and training

The following presentations and supporting papers presentations informed the discussions:

ESOL Provision at Leicester College, Peter Jones, Director of Curriculum, Leicester College.

LSC Funding Methodology and Approach, Geoff Daniels and Anita Hallam, LSC.

---

[1] See Annexe 3

London, Funding and Migration, Philippa Langton, LSC.

Migrant Workers, Sue Waddington, NIACE.

Migrant Workers – ESOL Committee of Inquiry, Mary Alys, TUC.

Good and Poor Quality ESOL Provision for Adult Learners, Alastair Pearson, Adult Learning Inspectorate.

Recommendations Arising from Inspections of the Curriculum Area of ESOL 2001–2006, Meena Wood, Ofsted.

The ESOL Effective Practice Project, Mike Baynham and Melanie Cooke, NRDC.

Paper on Teacher Education for the National Committee of Enquiry into ESOL, Helen Sunderland, LLU+.

Teacher Training and Professional Development in ESOL – Research, Helen Casey, NRDC.

Paper on the Reform of Teacher Training for the NIACE National Committee of Enquiry into ESOL, Paul Hambley, LLUK.

Advisory Board on Naturalisation and Integration (ABNI): Evidence to the ESOL Inquiry, Mary Coussey, ABNI.

Citizenship Materials for ESOL Learners, Chris Taylor, NIACE, Helen Sunderland, LLU+.

ESOL and Work, Jane Ward, NIACE.

Policy issues, Alan Tuckett, NIACE.

Written evidence

We received:
- 120 responses to our online questionnaire to inform the interim report (January–May 2006)[2]
- notes of
  - 63 written responses to our consultation on the interim report (May–August 2006)[3]
  - 51 responses to our teachers' survey (August 2006)[4]

Conferences

We spoke and/or ran workshops at the following conferences:

- 'More than a language...'. Launch of the ESOL Inquiry Interim report, May 2006
- NIACE Migrant Workers conference, February 2006
- Working to Rebuild Lives – One year on where are we now?, March 2006
- NATECLA National Conference, 2006
- Refugee Integration Conference, June 2006

Consultation meetings

- Asset Skills
- Department for Education and Skills

---

[2] see questionnaire Annexe 2.3
[3] see questionnaire Annexe 2.4
[4] see questionnaire Annexe 2.5

- Department for Work and Pensions
- EQUAL Healthcare ESOL Development Partnership project
- Jobcentre Plus
- Learning and Skills Council
- Learners – 11 focus groups were carried out by sector colleagues on our behalf (January–May 2006)
- NIACE
- Regional ESOL events in the North East, Yorkshire and Humber, North West, West Midlands, South East, London
- Two meetings with awarding bodies attended by:
  - Cambridge ESOL
  - City & Guilds
  - Edexcel
  - NOCN
  - OCN LR
  - Trinity College, London
- Two meetings convened by the Association of Colleges attended by:
  - Association of Colleges
  - Birmingham College
  - City of Bristol College
  - Dudley College of Technology
  - East Berkshire College
  - Lewisham College
  - Loughborough College
  - Nelson and Colne College
  - Tower Hamlets College
  - Westminster Kingsway College

2.3 NIACE Committee of Inquiry into English for Speakers of other Languages (ESOL)

Consultation questionnaire

Name

Job title

Organisation

Email address

Telephone number

The following questions relate to the committee's 5 main areas of focus. Please feel free to respond to any or all of the questions. Alternatively please explain your primary concerns regarding ESOL with any strategies you would like to suggest for addressing these issues. It would be helpful if, where relevant, you provide brief examples to illustrate issues you raise.

Definition: we are using the term ESOL to include all provision for speakers of other languages. This covers all settings where teaching and learning takes place, and encompasses language support to enable learners to access other subjects as well as designated language learning provision.

1. What is ESOL?

1a   How is ESOL defined in your organisation and what is its range and purpose?

1d   How does ESOL relate to EFL, do you treat them differently and, if so, how?

1c   What are the current demands for English language provision in your area? (What groups of speakers of other languages, what types of provision and support do they want or need?)

1d   To what extent are the language learning priorities identified in Q1c met? What are the main gaps, if any?

2. Leadership and management

2a   What is your organisation's vision of successful English provision for speakers of other languages? How is this vision implemented? What are the strongest features of this vision? Are there any weaknesses? How do you think it might be improved?

2b   Which policy, planning and funding priorities influence strategic thinking and planning in relation to ESOL in your organisation?

2c   How are managers and practitioners trained, inspired, supported and encouraged in their work with ESOL learners?

2d   What should the committee recommend to make leadership and management of ESOL more effective?

3. Quality

3a   What does inspirational and effective ESOL teaching, learning and language support look like in your view?

3b   To what extent do current approaches to initial, formative and summative assessment, Individual Learning Plans (ILPs) and teaching and learning strategies, support successful learning?

3c   Is the current accreditation and qualifications framework helpful for ESOL learners? How could it be better?

3d   To what extent do current approaches to providing information, advice and guidance and counselling meet learners' needs?

3e   What should the committee recommend to improve the quality of
(1)   ESOL teaching and learning?
(2)   Information, advice and guidance?

4. Teacher training and continuing professional development

4a   How are new ESOL tutors in your organisation recruited and supported to succeed on training programmes and is this effective?

4b   What does high quality, inspirational ESOL teacher training and continuing professional development look like?

4c To what extent does current Level 3 and 4 ESOL tutor training meet the needs of new and experienced tutors?

4d What should the committee recommend to ensure that the structures, approaches and content of initial teacher training and ongoing professional development equip the workforce to support ESOL learners to succeed?

5. Funding

5a What ESOL provision does your organisation offer and which funding streams are used to support it? What are benefits and/or disadvantages of these funding streams?

5b Is there sufficient funding to enable speakers of other languages to access ESOL provision that is responsive to their needs and priorities?

5c In your experience are some groups of students and/or employers willing and/or able to pay for ESOL?

5d How might ESOL be funded in the future to meet the language learning needs and priorities of all speakers of other languages?

6. Is there anything else you would like to tell us?

7. Would you be willing for us to contact you to ask you to provide further information or to discuss your responses?

Please return completed questionnaires to jane.ward@niace.org.uk or giustine.kettle@niace.org.uk

We will collect evidence until the end of May 2006 but responses by the end of <u>March 2006</u> will be particularly helpful if we are to have time to consider fully what you say.

2.4 NIACE Committee of Inquiry into English for Speakers of other Languages (ESOL)

Guidance for focus groups to gather evidence from adult speakers of other languages (5 pages)

The committee wants to take into account the views of adult speakers of other languages who want to develop their language skills. We are keen to hear from people who are not yet involved in learning as well as current learners.

We are collecting this evidence through focus groups. Focus groups are an efficient way of collecting information because they can provide a richer source of information than individual interviews. They can provide different perspectives, the group discussion can spark off new ideas and thoughts in participants and facilitators, and participants may jog each others' memories. Focus groups can benefit participants, as they feel more relaxed when with their peers and can learn from each other. Group interviews like this can give people a voice in developments and help participants develop and clarify their own ideas.

Questionnaires can exclude people who do not have the literacy or language skills to complete them. However, we would be pleased to receive written testimonies from adults you work with who prefer to communicate with us in this way. Please ask them to send to jane.ward@niace.org.uk or giustine.kettle@niace.org.uk

We will collect evidence until the end of May 2006 but responses by the end of <u>March 2006</u> will be particularly helpful if we are to have time to consider fully what you say.

Guidelines for focus groups

Aim

The aim of the focus group discussions is to elicit information and views on participants' backgrounds, motivations and aspirations, language learning priorities, preferred approaches to teaching and learning, qualifications, progression and funding. The emphasis of the discussions will be different for current learners and adults not currently taking part in learning.

Preparing for the session

- Identify two facilitators if possible as this makes it easier to make sure that all participants are included and to record the discussion.
- Both facilitators should know the group context.
- Use the discussion framework to prepare the session and think about how to adapt the language for your group (see pages 4 and 5 for frameworks for learners and adults who are not yet engaged in learning).
- Recruit 6–8 group participants.
- Agree strategies for ensuring all are able to contribute – we are not able to fund interpreters but you might be able to use student peers or staff to interpret in the sessions.
- Decide how you will record the session – tape or digital recording provides a full record but transcription is very time consuming. Taking notes in the session is more realistic in terms of time demands but means something might be missed. You could tape the session in order to use the tape as reference to check that written notes include all the important points.

At the beginning of the session

- Explain the purpose of the session, what areas it will cover and how long it will last.
- Ensure that everyone consents to participate – you might like to use or adapt the attached form.
- Ask for permission to tape and/or take notes.
- Explain that the meeting record will be sent to the committee and we will use the information in our report.
- Discuss anonymity – ask participants whether they would like to use their names or choose a different name for the record.

During the session

- You might like to use visuals or student writing as prompts to stimulate discussion.
- Use different types of questions:
  - Closed questions are useful to find out factual information, for example, 'When did you join this class?'
  - Open questions are useful to stimulate participants to talk about and reflect on their experiences and express their opinions and attitudes – ask for examples to clarify the focus
  - Probing questions can be used to explore an answer in more depth, e.g. Could you tell me more about …?' They can also be used to clarify an ambiguous answer, for example, ' Please could you explain…'
- Notice and respond to non verbal clues.
- Use positive reinforcement.
- Avoid telling participants what to say but clarify or pose options if they are not sure what the question means.
- Bring participants back to the question if they go too far off the point.
- Encourage under/non participants and manage over-participants.
- Take notes – use the question framework to structure the notes. Take down key points and quotes where possible.

At the end

- Emphasise the value and importance of everyone's contributions and thank them for taking part.

After the session

- Facilitators check the notes to make sure that all learners views are included, with quotes where available.
- Send the session notes to jane.ward@niace.org.uk

Discussion framework: current learners

The main question in bold is followed by prompts to support more detailed exploration. These areas might not all be relevant for every individual or group and it is likely that additional or different issues will emerge. Please adapt the language to suit the students you are working with.

Please note:

- The learning situation (e.g. type of ESOL class/language support, venue e.g. college, community, workplace, custodial setting)
- Summarise the group profile (ethnic group, gender, reasons/length of time living in UK, languages, education and employment histories, English language skills, current employment)

1. **Why are you learning English?**
- short /long term aspirations
- work
- family
- community

2. **What language classes do you attend?**
- Is it the days, times, content you want?
- What do you want to be able to do by the end of your course?

3. **What do you do in your class/language support session?**
- What have you learned so far?
- What activities help you learn most and why? (Probe speaking, listening, reading, writing activities, what the tutor does, resources they use.)
- How quickly have you learned?
- Are you satisfied with this?
- What would you change and how?

4. **What accreditation/ qualifications, if any, are you working towards?**
- How did you decide to do this?
- Is it what you want?
- How does it help you?

5. **Do you know what course you will do next?**
- How will you find out?

6. **Would you/your employers (if applicable) be willing to pay for learning?**
- What, if anything, could you afford?

Discussion framework: speakers of other languages not participating in learning

The main question in bold is followed by areas to explore in more detail. Please adapt the language to suit the adults you are working with.

Please note the:
- situation (e.g. community, workplace, custodial setting)
- group profile (ethnic group, gender, reasons/length of time living in UK, languages, education and employment histories, English language skills, current employment)

1. **Would you like to learn English and why?**
- short /long term aspirations
- work
- family
- community

2. **What kind of language classes would you like to attend?**
- type of course (English language/subject with language support)
- focus, content
- days, times, venue
- Do you know where to go/how to find out about provision?

3. **What stops you going to classes?**
- Available classes not what want
- Don't know how to find out what is on offer
- Time
- Cost
- What would help you to access English language classes?

4. **Would you/your employers (if applicable) be willing to pay for learning?**
- What, if anything, could you afford?

2.5 'More than a language…'

NIACE Committee of Inquiry into English for Speakers of other Languages (ESOL)

Consultation on the Interim report

Our interim report sets out the main issues that we have identified in relation to ESOL provision, and indicates our preliminary views on the ways in which they might be addressed. We would welcome your comments to help us refine our thinking and strengthen our recommendations.

Name...

Job title..

Organisation ....

Email address...

Telephone number..

Please focus your comments on the aspects of the report in which you have a particular interest or expertise, although you are of course welcome to respond to the full report. **(If you require extra space please write your answers on a separate sheet of paper.)**

1. The 5 main areas of focus in the report:

1. What is ESOL and why is it important?

2. Quality

3. Teacher training

4. Leadership and management

5. Funding

1.1 Have we identified the key issues correctly?

....

....

....

....

....

....

1.2 Have we made the right recommendations? If not, what alternatives do you suggest?

....

....

....

....

2. We would also welcome your views and suggestions about the issues we wish to consider in more depth (if you have not already discussed them in your response to the previous section).

2.1 What are the important factors?

....

....

....

....

....

....

2.2 What strategies would you suggest for addressing these issues?

ESOL and work, including the role of employers
ESOL and citizenship
ESOL language support for vocational learners in ESOL literacy classes
ESOL literacy

....

....

....

....

....

and further examination of

- quality issues
- qualifications issues
- the career structure for ESOL teachers
- the challenges for leadership and management
- funding issues.

....

....

....

....

Please send your responses to Jane Ward jane.ward@niace.org.uk or Giustine Kettle giustine.kettle@niace.org.uk before 31 July 2006.

NIACE
21 De Montfort Street
Leicester
LE1 7GE
Tel 0116 204 7067
Fax 0116 285 4514

3

Comparison of approaches to language learning for migrants in different countries

We have carried out web-based research into approaches to providing ESOL in other UK and major anglophone countries, and language learning for migrants in other European countries. This is presented in this annexe in three tables: Table 1: ESOL in the UK (not including England); Table 2: ESOL in major anglophone countries; Table 3: Language learning for migrants in European countries.

Table 1: ESOL in the UK (not including England)

	Programme	Entitlement	What purpose of learning?	Who is covered?	Expenditure	Number of people	Comments
Northern Ireland	Skills strategy	Free, some learners pay registration fee, £10–20. Course lengths vary.	'Essential skills for living' policy – skills to work.	Migrant workers, asylum seekers and refugees.	Unknown – Skills for Life budget	April to June 2005 3726 learners enrolled. Significant increase in the last two years.	2002 report identified ESOL as 'incoherent and patchy', limited resources and support available. Problems with mixed ability classes, needing eight people for class to start and students being reallocated to basic skills classes. Mentions the need for more than 72 hours tuition a year.
Scotland	ESOL (4/5ths in FE colleges)	Funding not always appropriate to learner needs. Mainly free places in community education provision (average in UK 15.5 months long). Fee-paying (international students) and free students mixed in same classes.	Participate in Scottish life (and employment).	Asylum seekers and refugees EU nationals settling in Scotland.	£5.4m for ESOL 2001–4. Some employers willing to pay. (Elsewhere says 2003–6 committed additional £1.7m a year to meet demand.) Different ways to obtain funding for ESOL.	9000 learners in 900 classes or home tutor 2003–4. Waiting lists exist.	Funding under Adult Literacy and Numeracy Partnership. Until 2005 data patchy and largely limited to Glasgow. 2005 mapping exercise. Volunteers play important role. Community-based ESOL classes are normally exempt from fees. Colleges either have sliding scale or waive fees for students on benefits or low-income. Asylum seekers and their families are exempt from fees for full-time and part time ESOL. EU students qualify for free part-time ESOL if deemed to be in Scotland to settle and not for educational purposes. National ESOL strategy is being developed.
Wales	In Basic Skills Strategy, delivery by BSA Wales	National Support Project for ESOL and English as an Additional Language planned (£120,000 earmarked for project in 2006–7).	All-age approach, have ten horizontal themes and ten priority groups.		Agency budget 2005–6 £11.5million, (£12.8m for 2006–7).		This applies to Basic Skills Strategy only – there are likely to be other resources allocated to ESOL across other Assembly Departments. Too early to estimate who will benefit from new project which covers newcomers and not migrants who have been in the UK for a long time.

Table 2: ESOL in major anglophone countries

	Programme	Entitlement	Requirements	What purpose of learning?	Who is covered?	Expenditure	Number of people	Comments
Australia	The Adult Migrant English Program (AMEP)	510 hrs free. Extra 100 hrs available for refugees (through Special Preparatory Program). Childcare.	Able to choose from selection of courses.	To settle successfully in Australia, 'functional' English.	Migrants and refugees, 18+ yrs.	AMEP budget 2004–5 $137.4 million.	2002 – tuition to over 32,000 clients.	Programme provided by Commonwealth Government through Dept. of Immigration and Multicultural Affairs (DIMA). Different forms of delivery; including 'It's over to you' ESOL delivered at home – for those who can't attend classes. Have AMEP research centre, which holds forums, conferences and professional development.
Canada	Language Instruction for Newcomers 'LINK' Federal programme	Free French/ ESOL for three yrs. Subsidised childcare / transport. Amount of training depends on need.	Immigrants able to choose most suitable course.	Everyday English/ French to participate in society. Lessons focus on learner needs.	All immigrants, and non-Canadian citizens (includes refugees) 18+ yrs.	2003–4 C$92 million Est. C$ 109.7 million 2005–6. Rising to 131 million 2007–8.	Have waiting lists. 2002 total immigrants and refugee 'landings' was 229,091.	Can be referred to other classes (may be fee involved). Any funding signed for a period of 12 months. Use Canadian Language Benchmark Assessment (CLBA stage 1). Aim to have classes where students are at the same level. Promote finding help in local community to access services, etc. Training provided by local community provision.

Table 2: Continued

	Programme	Entitlement	Requirements	What purpose of learning?	Who is covered?	Expenditure	Number of people	Comments
New Zealand	'English for migrants'	Pre-purchased courses, any extra costs student needs to pay. Three (and 3.5) years to take course.	Pre-paid (amount depends on ability – in some cases as much as $NZ 6650).	Some people need English for residency in NZ. Participate in society.	(Mainly skilled/ business). Migrants 16+ yrs.	None – charges also include admin costs.	1998–2004, 27 per cent of those eligible to purchase ESOL did (12,558 out of 46,256).	ESOL from Tertiary Education Commission (TEC). Majority of courses less than six months, most take between one and five courses. Sixty-three per cent of those who had pre-purchased had used some or all of tuition. Of those that had expired 84 per cent fully used entitlement, although rate is falling.
	Refugee study grants	Free places at approved courses.	Refugee.	Participate in society.	Refugees.			
	Academic migrant grants	Free places at approved courses.	Need tertiary qualification.		Some migrants.			
	Bilingual Tutor grants	Training to be ESOL tutor, 60 hours.	Bilingual language skills.	Receive Certificate.	Volunteer tutor.			25 schemes.
USA	Centre for Adult English Language Acquisition (CAELA).	To build infrastructure and support states with ESL* populations.	Provides ESL resources to states		Practitioners and planners.	40–50 per cent federal adult education. Programme funding has been used for ESL. Only some cases are federally funded	Based on 2000 census, est. 15 million adults would benefit from ESL courses. Demand outstrips supply.	Office of Vocational and Adult Education (OVAE) supports CAELA. Cannot find any info on specific programme or right to ESOL. Believe ESOL comes under Adult Education and Literacy System (AELS). Over 1400 sites offer ESL as well as NGOs and other education providers.

*ESL – English as a Second Language.

Table 3: Language learning for migrants in European countries

	Policy/ programme	Entitlement	Requirements	What purpose of learning?	Who is covered?	Expenditure	Number of people	Comments
Austria	Integration Agreements measurement since 2003.	75-hour language civilisation course (100 x 45-minute units). Course has three modules. Aim for level A1. Ongoing assessment. State reimburses 50 per cent of course costs up to a total limit of €182 if course completed within 18 months. If longer then only 25 per cent reimbursed The trainee pays average €80	For those below German language Level A1* When sign residency permit accept integration contract for one year. Initially sit 20-minute language test to see if exempt from course. If refuse to participate welfare benefit can be stopped and residency permit reduced.	Promotes linguistic assimilation (critics complain to the detriment of complete integration and promotion of employment).	Foreign nationals entering Austria lawfully with a view to long-term settlement. Foreigners in Austria since 1998 without permanent residency permit.	Courses cost €200 to €1000, each training organisation can set own fee.	15–20 per cent foreign nationals (others have sufficient level of German). 9000 people complied with contract in 2003. June 2004: 2000 had fulfilled contract by having lessons or passing test.	Training organisations are private contractors approved by Austrian Funds for Integration. No specific training required for teachers who are often volunteers. Local communities/associations may contribute to the expenses. If not exempt and language course not started within 3 years must pay state €200, after 4 years have residency permit revoked unless valid justification. 75 hours sufficient for 90% to attain level A1.* Child minding problems result in low participation by women.

* Of the Common European Framework of Reference for Languages.

Table 3: Continued

	Policy/programme	Entitlement	Requirements	What purpose of learning?	Who is covered?	Expenditure	Number of people	Comments
Denmark	1998 Integration Law, each Local Authority responsible for Entry Programme for new arrivals and refugees. 2003 Act to add asylum seekers to the Law.	Free: State pays tuition for up to three years. Includes language instruction, Danish society and training courses. Immigrants must follow course for 30 hours per week for six months (unless working). Fewer hours for 17–25-year-old asylum seekers. Each six-monthly module validated by test.	To be foreigner officially registered with municipality. Immigrant obliged to enter contract with local authority in first month into country for welfare benefits and permanent resident status. Participation enables asylum seekers to claim all of their benefits.	Explicit objective is integration. To use Danish 'actively and creatively' in daily lives, work or study. To obtain Danish nationality must have spoken Danish between level B1 and B2* and written B1.	All foreigners officially registered with municipality.	Cost of entry programme €120m for language tuition) paid by state to local authority. Average cost of €18,000 per person	Approx. 46,000 immigrants were trained in 2003. The system has an absence rate of around 25 per cent. Local authorities may run language courses or sub-contract to public or private organisations.	Local authorities are responsible for quality of instruction. Teachers must have adequate professional qualifications in teaching Danish as a foreign language for a year in addition to other training. There are about 1,600 teachers and about 50 language centres.
France	Reported in 2004: plans to create National Agency for Entry and Migration under the Employment Labour and Social Cohesion Ministry. Funded through state 'Fund for action and support for integration and combating discrimination'.	Free: State pays language course (200-500 hrs – 6-30 hrs/wk) as part of 'Contract of welcome and integration', also have modules on life in France. Receive Oral proficiency Cert. Assessed every 3 months.	Can choose to sign Integration Contract but once signed it is obligatory. Lasts for 1 year, can be renewed for another year.	Acquisition of basic spoken language skills (level A1*). Oral proficiency, used for citizenship.	Immigrants	Cost of entry programme funded entirely by state.	90 per cent of immigrants sign contract but not all have language needs	The language courses are not sufficient for daily life. Solution is for employers to provide language courses. Tuition must be flexible and accessible.

* Of the Common European Framework of Reference for Languages.

Table 3: Continued

	Policy/ programme	Entitlement	Requirements	What purpose of learning?	Who is covered?	Expenditure	Number of people	Comments
Germany	New immigration law adopted July 2004, started Integration Programme.	300-hour language module (renewable once, 600-hour maximum) plus 30 hours civic and social instruction. Sit test to obtain Level B1 (oral + written).* Immigrants contribute maximum €1/hour.	New immigrants' right to participate lasts for two years. Non-participation can result in 10 per cent reduction in welfare benefits.	To integrate into German society. Drive to have skilled immigrants as poorly qualified immigrants can have negative social consequences.	New immigrants and settled foreigners (if places available).	€230m	Have 50,000 to 60,000 places available per year.	Immigrants sit initial test to see whether exempt (higher than Level B1) from the courses. The focus is on quality and ensuring skilled immigrants. Language tuition organisations tender for funding. 140 hours additional teacher training is available. In 2002 ran pilot project – 9 month intensive course. Vouchers used at approved language courses (up to 900 hrs), subsidised childcare. The pilot was mandatory to all new immigrants in the area. During pilot 3,385 vouchers were distributed.
Netherlands	Since 1998 newcomers language courses. Since 2000 'old comers' also need to attend language courses. Integration of Newcomers Act to be established in 2006: 'New Entry Programme'.	In 1990s 600-hour language training, 600-hour society and LM orientation. Integration programme lasts three years. Must sit test and achieve level A2.* The State reimburses the student up to 50 per cent of the costs when they pass the language exam (2006).	New immigrants obliged. Municipalities to have contract with any immigrant to specify obligations, terms and sanctions.	To be professionally and socially independent to participate in society. Focus on oral skills.	New immigrants (more recently old immigrants), includes refugees.	€6000 per person (2002).	30,000 newcomers in 2003, of which 23,000 obliged to do integration course (77 per cent). Long-term settled foreigners (approx. 460,000) may also benefit with no obligation to participate.	Long waiting lists, low effectiveness and unclear information packages. Justice Ministry is responsible for entry policy. A commission determines the level of tests and chooses the subjects. The state has signed agreements with vocational training bodies to enable unemployed new comers to use acquired language skills in a professional context.

* Of the Common European Framework of Reference for Languages.

Table 3: Continued

	Policy/ programme	Entitlement	Requirements	What purpose of learning?	Who is covered?	Expenditure	Number of people	Comments
Spain	1985 Act relating to education rights.	Entitled to free courses, duration unlimited. Specific teachers offer language courses to those who need them. Not systematically tested.	All population entitled to free courses. Not obligatory.		New immigrants.	Interior and Education ministries finance free language courses.		1215 state adult education schools in Spain that offer language courses. While not systematically tested learner can receive certificate through training courses. Foreign language teachers have access to teacher training which is free and paid training.
Sweden	Swedish Tuition for Immigrants (SFI) – municipalities responsible for SFI.	Free provision. Seems to be unlimited hours.		Language proficiency and knowledge. Swedish society to fulfil citizen obligations. Grades awarded (Pass and Pass with credit).	Immigrants and Finnish nationals near border who work in Sweden.		Large increase in number of immigrants.	Government decides curriculum, where possible combined with work experience or volunteering opportunities. 2006 new proposals – includes creation of Language Council. OECD thematic review highlights poor quality of SFI and lack of tutors. Need more holistic and integrated approach.

* Of the Common European Framework of Reference for Languages.

Acronyms used in this report

A8	Accession countries to the European Union (EU)
ACL	Adult and community learning
ALI	Adult Learning Inspectorate
APEL	Accreditation of Prior Experience and Learning
BEGIN	Basic Educational Guidance in Nottinghamshire
CACHE	Council for Awards in Children's Care and Education
CBI	Confederation of British Industry
CEL	Centre for Excellence in Leadership
Cert. Ed./PGCE	Certificate in Education/Postgraduate Certificate in Education
COIC	Commission on Integration and Cohesion
CPD	Continuing professional development
CSR	Comprehensive Spending Review
DfES	Department for Education and Skills
DWP	Department for Work and Pensions
EFL	English as a foreign language
EQUAL	Employment initiative funded through ESF
ESF	European Social Fund
ESOL	English for Speakers of Other Languages
ETP	Employer Training Pilots (now Train to Gain)
EU	European Union
FE	Further education
FENTO	Further Education National Training Organisation (now LLUK)
GCSE	General Certificate of Secondary Education
HE	Higher education
HEFCE	Higher Education Funding Council for England
HEIs	Higher education institutions
IAG	Information, advice and guidance
ICT	Information and communication technology

IELTS	International English Language Testing System
ILEA	Inner London Education Authority
ILP	Individual Learner Plan
ILR	Individual Learning Record
ILT	Industrial Language Training
JCP	Jobcentre Plus
LDA	London Development Agency
LLN	Literacy, language and numeracy
LLU+	London Language and Literacy Unit
LLUK	Lifelong Learning UK
LSC	Learning and Skills Council
LSO	Learner Support Organiser
LSU	London Strategic Unit for the Learning and Skills Workforce
Matrix	Qualification standards for information, advice and guidance
NATECLA	National Association for Teachers of English and other Community Languages to Adults
NHS	National Health Service
NIACE	National Institute of Adult Continuing Education
NQF	National Qualifications Framework
NRDC	National Research and Development Centre for Adult Literacy and Numeracy
Ofsted	Office for Standards in Education
PRLS	Professional Recognition Learning and Skills Scheme
PSA	Public Service Agreement
QCA	Qualifications and Curriculum Authority
QIA	Quality Improvement Agency
RARPA	Recognising and recording progress and achievement
SfL	Skills for Life
SMART	Specific, Measurable, Achievable, Realistic, Time-related
SSC	Sector Skills Council
SVUK	Standards Verification UK
TESOL	Teacher of English to Speakers of Other Languages
T to G	Train to Gain
TUC	Trades Union Congress